the Miraculous
everyday

by Alison Elliot

COVENANTERS' PRESS

First published in 2005 by
Scottish Christian Press
An imprint of the Board of Parish Education of the Church of Scotland
21 Young Street, Edinburgh EH2 4HU

A catalogue record for this publication is available from the British Library.

ISBN 1904325351

Cover design by Context Edinburgh
Layout by Heather Macpherson
Editor: Johnston McKay

Alison is the Associate Director of Edinburgh University's Centre for Theology and Public Issues, and an Honorary Fellow of New College. Originally trained in mathematics and linguistics, she became an academic child psychologist and lectured at Lancaster and Edinburgh Universities. Always interested in church and society and ecumenical issues, Alison was convener of the Church of Scotland's Church and Nation Committee, is a member of the Central Committee of the Conference of European Churches and is convener of the Scottish Churches' Forum, the principal representative body for the nine mainstream Scottish Churches that constitute ACTS (Action of Churches Together in Scotland). She has held a number of civic appointments. Alison is an Elder of Greyfriars Tolbooth and Highland Kirk in the City of Edinburgh. She was made an OBE in 2003 and has been awarded honorary degrees by Trinity College Dublin, Knox College Toronto and the Universities of Edinburgh and St Andrews.

CONTENTS

INTRODUCTION

One of the great pleasures this year has been the chance to share worship with people. And what has made that a special pleasure is that this was the part of the role of Moderator that worried me most at the start. Not being trained in preaching, I was anxious about people expecting me to take on the same preaching load as my predecessors. But people were patient and gave me the chance to offer a reflection during the service in my own way. Over the year, this became something I looked forward to; the privilege of sharing with others the tremendous range of experiences that the Moderator's year affords; and the opportunity to stretch my understanding of the Christian faith as I reflected on these experiences within the discipline of worship.

This book brings together some of the prayers, addresses and talks that I gave during the year. During the General Assembly, it is the responsibility of the Moderator to lead worship at the start of each day's proceedings and to preach in St Giles on the Sunday. Each day, I chose a psalm and Bible readings appropriate to the business that was to follow and, after a short piece for 'cello and sometimes flute, we joined in prayer. These choices are spread throughout the book.

If the Moderator is invited to take part in a service, it's generally for a special occasion and I've included some of the addresses and prayers that I wrote for these events. Several of these are fixtures in the diary; the National War Memorial Service; the service in the crypt in the Palace of Westminster; Crathie, in the presence of the Royal Family and the Prime Minister. Others were particular to the year: the tenth anniversary of the ordination of women in the Scottish Episcopal Church; Founder's Day at George Watson's College in Edinburgh; the school my children had attended. And there were lots of anniversaries for congregations, of which St Andrew's Toronto is one example. The church year offers several special festivals and I was asked to take part in services on Christmas Day, Remembrance Day and Palm Sunday. I have also grouped separately various writings and talks that I gave after visiting Sri Lanka and South India, in the wake of the terrible disaster of the tsunami in the Indian Ocean. We had already planned to visit North India at the start of January, so altered our plans to go to some of the affected areas about ten days after the tragedy. The Scotsman article was sent home while we were still in Sri Lanka and the addresses given in St Andrew's and Glasgow followed shortly after we arrived home.

Sometimes, you are asked to give a talk that is surrounded by worship, rather than an address that is central to it. The Annual Guild Meeting was a splendid occasion in the Glasgow Concert Hall (and I was made particularly welcome at it). So too was the event in Knox Theological College in Toronto, part of their 160th anniversary celebrations. Both provided an opportunity to speak more extensively than is possible in a service and I've included versions of each talk.

These prayers and addresses have grown in a rich soil of experience and friendship. Throughout my year as Moderator, I've been inspired and supported by Jo, my generous and patient husband, Richard, my ever-encouraging minister, and my excellent chaplains, Johnston and Sheilagh, who have gone to great lengths to make the year easy for me. We have shared insights about our faith, reflected on what we were discovering, and I want to thank them warmly for being such marvellous companions.

Alison Elliot, Easter Day 2005.

BROAD LIKE BEACH AND MEADOW
Luke 24: 28-3; Psalm 84

Your love, O God, is broad like beach and meadow
It spreads its warmth and its strength over the whole
inhabited world.
It searches out the hesitant, the self deprecating, the self
obsessed and beckons them into its embrace.
It makes space for the awkward customers, for the
forgotten, the embarrassing and the downright anti-social.
And we each hear ourselves called by name and dignified
by your particular attention.
And you give us peace.

Your love, O God, shows up the narrowness of our own.
Our fastidiousness in preserving our own purity at the
expense of others' need
The presumptuousness of the barriers we erect against
true fellowship
The busyness that blinkers us to the gift of the precious
moment
Our forgetfulness and our false priorities.

Lord, have mercy
Christ have mercy
Lord, have mercy

Gracious God,
Grant that your love will so fill our hearts and guide our
actions
That our fear and introversion will give way to an
exuberant generosity that is worthy of your children.

Your love, O God, brings out the best in us
We offer you things of great beauty
Intricate embroidery, mellifluous music, carvings in wood
or stone that delight and instruct
And buildings.
    Beautiful buildings.
    New buildings.
    Large buildings.
    Historic buildings that speak to us of the faith and
    sometimes the folly of the past.
And we treasure them.

Loving God, we understand the dangers of becoming
walled up
    in our churches,
    in our history,
    in our tradition.

Remind us of the gifts that the stranger brings
And guide us, we pray, in our deliberations today,
That your church may be
A sanctuary and a shrine for all people,

A place of strength for the weak
Of refuge for the troubled
Where the hospitality of your love radiates so that all can
share it
We ask this in the name of your welcoming son, our
Saviour, Jesus Christ. Amen

*Saturday May 15th 2005, for the discussion at the General Assembly
following reports from the Panel on Doctrine, the Board of Stewardship
and Finance and the General Trustees.*

A FUTURE OF PROMISE AND POSSIBILITY

Let me take you to Strasbourg. A beautiful old city that sits right on one of the fault lines of Europe, on the boundary between France and Germany. Over the years, it has been traded backwards and forwards between them. Today, it is home to the European Court of Human Rights, the European Parliament, the Council of Europe, each in its own way trying to help the peoples and the nations of Europe to rise above their ancient hatreds.

Three years ago, it was the setting for a large church gathering and I was there. At one point we visited the Council of Europe. And some people were specially invited to talk about what their faith meant to them and to offer a symbol of this to the rest of us.

First off the mark was Vlad, a Greek Catholic from Romania who plonked a battered sandal on the desk. He was a youth worker in his twenties. He talked about the excitement of hearing the Christian message for the first time when he was fifteen and about the journey he had travelled since then.

Then there was Margarethe. She's Dean of Västerås Cathedral in Sweden. She offered a carafe of clear water and spoke about her experience as a woman in the church.

But the story that stayed with me came from John. English, very Anglican, an official with the Council of Europe. I don't remember what symbol he offered, but I do remember what he said. He said that the most important thing about his Christian faith was that it helped him and his colleagues to cope with the failures and frustrations of their jobs: not just the day-to-day frustrations of the photocopier not working.

He was talking about the deep frustrations of working in an organisation that had high ideals, yet had to carry on living with the everyday experience of having to settle for less; of living continually in that gap between aspiration and achievement; of living in that "two steps forward, one step back" kind of world that is so familiar to people in public or professional life, and, of course, to people in the church.

So let's take time this morning to consider that gap between the world we long for and the world we find ourselves in. How does our faith help us to cope with it?

Moses found himself literally contemplating the distance between the world he hoped for and where he had got to. He now knew that he would never reach the Promised Land, although he was allowed to see it. He had been an odd choice as leader of his people but they had followed him through all kinds of adventures and setbacks. His life had been one of cajoling, pleading, negotiating, placed uncomfortably between God and his recalcitrant people. Yet he was always spurred on by the vision and the promise of a land of peace and plenty. For him, that vision was not to be realised. But without it, they would still have been slaves in Egypt, or dispersed through the countries round about.

Moses was continually drawn into a future of promise. And this makes his life a model for a life of faith.

We too are people of faith and we too have our promises of a better future. As we are drawn into it, we are tempted to replace the promise or the vision with something less, with plans and protocols and blueprints but we must never take our eyes off the promise itself.

Today is World Debt Day, and today we lay claim to the promise of a world where the chains of debt are broken that keep the world's poor in poverty.

Today, the obscene legacy of war continues to destroy people in the Middle East, and today we lay claim to the promise of a world where justice and peace embrace one another.

Today, the deadly clock of HIV infection keeps ticking and today we lay claim to the promise of a world where all can have life in all its fullness.

Today, we grieve alongside the families and friends of the victims of the explosion in the Glasgow plastics factory last week, and today we lay claim to the promise that God will wipe away tears from all faces.

As people of faith, we are drawn into a future of promise.

But there's something one-dimensional about the kind of future that belies the abundant promise of Easter, because, as people of Easter, we are released into a future of possibility. Christ's resurrection has broken the chains that tie us to the fears of the past that constrain our future.

Iain Crichton Smith once did a spot of dreaming:

> I build an orange church and put inside it
> a little orange minister in a pulpit
> that's dandelion yellow.
> I make a ceiling of intensest blue.
> The seats are heliotrope, the bibles pink,
> hymn books are apple green.
> Picasso paints the walls with animals.
> The angels swoop in red and there's a sun
> of blinding nuclear light.

It might not be to your taste, but I warm to its exuberance, its reckless freshness, its unreality. But there's another verse.

> And so transform it all… But for the guilt
> that's small and black and creeps in when the door
> swings on its oiled hinges.

Iain Crichton Smith, Selected Poems

Is it guilt? Or fear of betraying the past? Or embarrassment at being seen to be different?

We can all give a name to the little black figure that holds *us* back from dreaming and imagining and living in this world of abundant possibility that the risen Christ releases us into.

At that same Strasbourg gathering, Cardinal Cormac Murphy O'Connor speculated on what it was that prevented real change from happening in the church. He made three suggestions – suspicion, inertia and impatience. Faults we can see in others. But in our own case, we dress them up in positive terms. *Others are suspicious.* We talk instead of the particular responsibility that's been entrusted to us and the need to discharge it ourselves. *Others suffer from inertia.* We talk of valuing and cherishing our fine religious heritage. *Others are impatient.* We argue that some things are too important to entrust to the scrutiny of others who wouldn't understand the urgency about them. So perhaps we should add self-deception to the list.

It's a terrible indictment of our resurrection hope that we use our imagination and our intellect so often to think up reasons for sticking with the well tried ways. Our life should be bursting with creativity, imagination, new ways of doing things. But is it?

As people of Easter, we are released into a future of possibility.

Of course, such a future can descend into chaos, or randomly grasping at novelty for its own sake. But as followers of Jesus Christ, we are guided by the Holy Spirit into uncharted territory.

I was thinking about the passage from St John's Gospel when we were on holiday recently in Crete. One day, we put on our hiking boots and set out across the hillside, clutching our *Landscapes of Western Crete* guidebook. Before we started, we noticed that the book had last been updated 13 years ago, so instructions to "turn left at the house with the barking guard dog" might no longer be much use.

But all went well, up onto the ridge, through the village to the viewpoint across to Rethymnon, along the path edged with waist-high sage. But then the path disappeared, under a forest of aggressive thorn bushes that made further progress impossible. End of country walk. Back to the main road and a long journey back to the car.

Written guidance is all very well but there are times when you need the immediacy of a living guide who knows what path is right for today's complexities.

A living guide is the gift that Christ promised his friends through the Holy Spirit. His direct teaching, through word and example, was soon to come to an end but it would be kept fresh and up to date as the Spirit helped his followers negotiate new territory in worlds they couldn't dream of at that time. They would find paths that others had dismissed. The ones "less travelled by", as Robert Frost has said: ones where peace and comfort were different things. "Peace I leave with you; my peace I give to you." Real peace, whose hallmark is justice, not a quiet life. Deep peace, enriched by God's vulnerable love.

This week, in the General Assembly, it's our task to look into the future. Will we be drawn forward by vision and promise? Will we allow ourselves to dream a little, of mustard seeds or salt or trumpets? Will we trust in the guiding presence of the Holy Spirit? Or will we see only the long shadow of yesterday's thorn thickets?

This morning, we are sharing this service with friends from other churches and from other parts of Scottish public life. And that reminds us that there's more at stake than the future of a church that's nurtured *us* and that we love dearly. We are the guardians of an important part of their heritage too. They share with us a commitment to costly service, care for the weak, integrity in our dealings with others. We bring with us a rich legacy of courage and risk. For everyone's sake, may we place that at the service of a future of promise, of possibility and of adventure.

Sunday 16th May 2005 at the General Assembly service in St Giles' Cathedral.

THE CHURCH'S MINISTRY

Ephesians 4:1-16, Psalm 68

Almighty God
Today we celebrate our Lord's ascension into heaven
The final scene of his earthly drama
And we imagine thrones and trumpets and music and
multitudes

But what we are told about is a cloud, a murky, wispy,
insubstantial cloud
That hid him so that he could be seen no more.

So today we celebrate the paradoxes of our faith.

The almighty God who abandoned his glory and became
a little child
The embodiment of truth who taught in fanciful stories
The Lord of life who submitted to death

Today, we celebrate the paradox of Christ's ascension
Removed from the sight of some, he becomes known to
us all through love
Plucked from the particularity of first century Palestine, he
reigns over all time and space
Moving out of the realm of knowledge and certainty, he
enters the cloudy realm of truth.
> And so empowers lives today that are his hands and
> feet
> and his eyes that look out compassionate on the
> world.

Lord Jesus

Today we pray for the church as it proclaims your truth

Celebrates your life and resurrection

And pursues its ministry of care and reconciliation

To the people of Scotland

We give thanks for the skill and dedication of those who serve you through the church

And for the ministries as yet untapped within our fellowship

We have the audacity to consider ourselves your body in today's world

Grant that we may lead lives infected with your justice,

Haunted by your peace

And bound together by your love.

This we ask in your name. Amen

Ascension Day 2004 (Thursday May 20th) when the General Assembly discussed ministry.

THE MESSAGE OF THE STONES:
Remembrance Day at the National War Memorial, Edinburgh Castle

It was Palm Sunday. Jesus was being hailed triumphantly by an ecstatic crowd as he rode into Jerusalem. And some of the Pharisees in the crowd said to him, 'Teacher, tell your disciples to stop'. And Jesus answered: 'I tell you, if they were silent the stones would shout out'

Some messages cannot be silenced. We think that, if we burn books, the ideas in them will disappear. We think that if we kill people, the passions they lived by will disappear. We think that, if we shut people away, they will be forgotten.

The National War Memorial is about the persistence of memory. And the eternal messages of war and peace. It stands in a remarkable tradition of attempts to give shape and permanence to a nation's memory of its collective, painful past.

Five years ago, I was privileged to visit Berlin, to record a radio programme about the ways in which that city remembered its past. Berlin has a complicated and painful history. It's difficult to keep track of which of its neighbours were friends, which enemies, at any particular point in its past. And it marks that past in a great variety of ways.

The Neue Wache is a small, round, classical building. Inside there's a beautiful modern Pieta of a strong woman cradling a soldier. It speaks of the human pain of war.

The Soviet War Memorial is massive, all heroic poses and military strength. It speaks of the defiant triumphalism of war.

The Kaiser Wilhelm Memorial Church has been left as a bombed ruin, its remaining tower pointing jaggedly up into the sky. It speaks of the destructiveness of war.

The Gestapo headquarters has been left as a kind of makeshift exhibition of newspaper cuttings, in a trench. It speaks of the shameful context of war.

So our memorials speak to us selectively out of the complexity and confusion of wartime, and communicate a particular message down the years, a message precious to those creating the memorial, a message for us to decode.

So what are these stones saying to us?

The most powerful message given by this building is the message that, even in wartime, individual people matter. Visitors come here from all round the world to look for the particular name of their grandfather, or their mother, or their son. If truth is the first casualty of war, the second must be the particularity of those at the heart of the drama.

Slavenka Drakulic, the Croatian writer, has recently completed a book about the War Crimes Tribunal in the Hague concerning the war in Former Yugoslavia. She makes the point that, at the start of the war, the names of the few soldiers and policemen killed were noticed, their photographs and names printed on the front pages of newspapers. But in the years that followed, when, as she says, it became a real war, death became an ordinary thing. Nobody bothered to list the names any more.

Warfare plays strange games with people's identity. A numbers mentality can take over. We contrast the casualty totals of each side, concentrating on how the figures stack up. And so we distance ourselves from the responsibility we owe to each person as a precious child of God, dignified with a unique identity. Or nowadays, we can conduct war geographically at a distance, focused on computer screens, again losing any sense of who it is that we're targeting. The logic of war reduces each person to the single label of friend or foe, in a complete denial of the specific love that God has for each of us.

That's why we have to seize every opportunity to resist the depersonalisation of war. As the American families did recently, when they insisted that people should see pictures of the coffins of their loved ones. It may have been inconvenient in political terms but no-one should be denied the right to their own identity, particularly in death.

That's why Remembrance Day is so important. If you know someone who was killed in war, and you remember family holidays you spent together or office parties when they told awful jokes, you are investing them again with the particular personhood that the logic of war denies people. It's interesting that in Rwanda, they've established a war memorial that includes stories about the people that died, listing children's favourite toys, or their first word, as well as their name.

And that's why this building is important. These records are a small act of dignity and respect that contributes to healing part of the violence that war has done to those commemorated here, and so to building peace.

A second message that strikes me in this building speaks about the binding power of service. The frieze in the Shrine captures the sense of the whole country on the move, with skills and backgrounds and lives put at the disposal of each other. It extends the picture away from the horrendous waste of the trenches, away from the propaganda of Kitchener's insistent finger, away from the callous collateral damage of today's conflicts. It invites us to believe in something noble, in the capacity of human beings to give up what is dear to them for the sake of some greater purpose. It reminds us of the lengths people have gone to, to protect each other, to look after those weaker than themselves, to save the land they love.

And our sceptical twenty-first century mind recoils from it. We know too much about the history, about the irresponsible shambles of the First World War. We see exploitation instead of commitment, a dangerous incipient nationalism rather than love of country. It's hard to communicate across the generations, across the Cold War, the Holocaust, the Geneva Conventions and the ethnic cleansing, and accept the sincerity of the service they offered each other.

Yet we demand that service of others. We still send troops to do our political bidding. We expect aid workers to put our donations to good use, to patch up the damage done by policies we have willed. We take it for granted that any conflict will be assiduously covered by the media. Yet, however well they report from the front, ours is still a dangerously disconnected culture. Warfare is carried out vicariously by others, to the point where it becomes possible to talk about war as pre-emptive action, to see war as one tool of foreign policy, rather than a desperate last resort.

Jesus wept over the city of Jerusalem. "If you had only recognised on this day the things that make for peace!" We still get it wrong. We confuse peace with quietness, with the ending of hostilities, rather than the continual search for justice and love and healing. We see peace as something we construct, not the gift Jesus gives to those who love him.

The people who built this memorial thought they'd cracked it. They *did* believe they'd just fought the war to end all wars. How else to make sense of the horror and grief they'd gone through? Looking back, they believed they'd won the war on war. And we smile bitterly. Because we envy them their naivety.

Yet today, we're embarking on the war, not on war, but on terror. What would these stones tell us about that undertaking? Stones that have continued to receive lists of the war dead for seventy-seven years since the memorial was opened. Would they speak to us of the triumph of military might or the enduring strength of comradeship and service? Of the power of the dramatic gesture or the value of eternal vigilance? Of mankind's right to total security or his essential vulnerability? Of hawks or of pelicans?

"Do not let your hearts be troubled. Believe in God, believe also in me. Peace I leave with you. My peace I give to you." Let us listen.

Some years ago, members of Carnwadric Parish Church in Glasgow wrote a hymn, which I'll end by quoting:

What shall we pray for those who died,
those on whose death our lives relied?
Silenced by war, but not denied,
God give them peace.

What shall we pray for those who mourn
friendships and love, their fruit unborn?
Though years have passed, hearts still are torn;
God give them peace.

What shall we pray for those who know
nothing of war, and cannot show
grief or regret for friend or foe?
God give them peace.

God give us peace and, more than this,
show us the path where justice is;
and let us never be remiss
working for peace that lasts.

*The annual service at the National War Memorial in Edinburgh Castle
on Thursday May 27th 2004.*

STANDING ON HOLY GROUND

Surely the Lord is in this place; and I knew it not.

God of hope and of peace
We pray for places made holy by your presence

Places of pain
Places of doubt
Places of healing

Compassionate God,
We pray for those whose suffering blots out thoughts of
you
     And of your mercy
Those living with the pain of terminal illness
     With the indignity of abuse
     With the terror of persecution
Those who feel abandoned
     By the rest of society in their poverty
     By neighbours and family in their old age
     By their loved ones as they mourn their death
Those whose lives are invaded
     by grief,
     by anger,
     by injustice

Come close to them, we pray, and grant that they might
know the power of your spirit
     To strengthen and protect them

Disturbing God

We pray for those who cannot accept the certainties of others

Who are alienated by a black and white world
that misses the colour and subtlety of the life they know

Who long to move towards the horizon of new possibility
But are clawed back into the world as it must be

Who see dim shapes beyond the reflections in the official looking glass

Guide them, we pray, through your singular world
where the only absolutes are the depth of your love and the strength of your truth

Nurturing God

We pray for those whose lives have been blessed by your healing touch
By a smile or a word that speaks of your care

We pray for neighbours, pastors, counsellors, passers-by
Who see the world through the lens of your encompassing love

We pray for politicians, lawyers, campaigners
Who are inspired by a vision of your generous justice

And we pray for ourselves and those we love
That we may know the wholesome peace of your gentle presence

Eternal God,

Whose love is not limited by time or space

At this season of Pentecost

We celebrate the coming of your Holy Spirit to the

disciples,

    fearful, confused, hurting

Grant that your Spirit's power may be at work within us

    energising us

    purifying us

    comforting us

releasing us into a future of peace, of justice and of reconciliation.

We ask this in the name of our risen, living Lord, Jesus Christ, Amen

Thursday June 2nd 2004, service on the Mull of Kintyre to mark the tenth anniversary of the Chinook helicopter crash.

ZACCHAEUS: A SMALL MAN

Isaiah 1: 10-18; Luke 19: 1-10

I was glad to see that the reading for this morning was the story of Zacchaeus. He's turning out to have quite a starring role in my year as Moderator. Our Department of Education decided that what I needed for the year was some material to use for children's addresses, so they put together for me a Story Sack, a wonderful big bag in red plush, with gold lining and huge gold tassels round it. Inside is a specially illustrated version of the story, a soft toy Jesus and a soft toy Zacchaeus, a glove in the form of a tree for Zacchaeus to sit in and a jigsaw. The children love it. The book is called, "Jesus goes for a sleep-over". For them, the emphasis in the story is on the importance of inclusion, even of people as unpopular as Zacchaeus.

But there are other messages in the story. The fact that it was with Zacchaeus that Jesus chose to stay on his visit to Jericho provokes questions for those who think that the church is only for people who are good and pure and pious and respectable. It's not. Jesus made a habit of searching out people on the edge of society, and the church should be doing the same.

And the fact that, at the end of the story, Zacchaeus makes amends for the extortion he has operated before his encounter with Jesus shows that we can't classify people into good and bad and leave it at that. Jesus didn't. His love can transform all kinds of lives.

But today I want to focus on an obvious feature of the story: Zacchaeus climbed the sycamore tree because he was a small man.

Now, when St Paul was writing to the Ephesians, he urged them to grow up to full manhood; to realise their true humanity, which, he says, is to be measured by nothing less than the full "stature" of Christ.

And in the Greek of the New Testament, the same word is used in Paul's phrase, "the full stature of Christ" as is used in Luke's description of Zacchaeus as "small in stature".

I wonder: if Paul didn't mean physical height when he spoke of measuring ourselves against "the full stature of Christ"... is it possible that Luke meant more than just a physical description of Zacchaeus when he says that he was a small man?

Maybe he meant to convey something more than a statement about Zacchaeus' height.

We don't know a lot about Zacchaeus, but from the little information we have we can gather quite a lot. And I suspect that there were three things about Zacchaeus which are typical of small men. Not small in height but small in outlook, in attitude, in approach.

First of all, I suspect Zacchaeus only wanted success, and so achieved nothing.

Mind you, that's not how it must have seemed on the surface. Zacchaeus lived in Jericho, and Jericho was the Monte Carlo or the Bermuda or the Maldives of Palestine. It was where rich people went for the winter. Every autumn, the court of King Herod uprooted itself from Jerusalem and settled in Jericho for the season. It was a place with warm swimming pools, and fertile parks and impressive villas, one of which probably belonged to Zacchaeus. He was a Superintendent of Taxes. He had gone up in the world. He was a success. Zacchaeus was a success, but because he had wanted success at any price, he was friendless and lonely, shunned and despised, avoided and beneath contempt. Because he only wanted success he actually achieved nothing.

And I suspect that Zacchaeus totally suppressed his past and so mortgaged his future.

You didn't have to be the most fervent Jewish nationalist to regard how Zacchaeus made his money as utterly despicable. Jewish people were proud people. They may have been overrun by a pagan empire, but at least they tried to keep their dignity and preserve their respect as Jewish people. And Zacchaeus managed to suppress all of that, to forget his Jewishness with its proud past and long traditions… and he did that so successfully that he was able to pretend to himself that there would never be a day of reckoning. But devout Jews would have had no doubt that he would have to answer for his collaboration with those who had crushed God's chosen people.

And thirdly, I suspect, Zacchaeus cynically used other people and so lost all respect.

In the Palestine of Jesus' days, people bought a tax franchise from the Roman authorities, who said "Pay me so much money for the right to gather taxes in a district, and you can charge what you like and the profit's yours". Zacchaeus would have paid a fairly hefty sum to the Romans for this franchise, and as far as they were concerned that was the end of the matter. It was up to Zacchaeus to extort as much as he could from the people in his area. It all went into his pocket. And the balance between what he paid for the franchise and what he collected from the people was his profit. People mattered to Zacchaeus, not for who they were or what they did but for what he could get out of them. He used people to build up his personal fortune. And he paid the price in the coinage of respect, for nobody had any respect for him at all - not the Jewish people from whom he extorted his profit, nor the Romans who despised him for the hack he was.

Zacchaeus was a small man. But before we criticise him too severely, don't we all share something of his attitude?

Don't we all imagine that there is something called "success" which is outside of ourselves and able to be measured and assessed and maybe even envied and admired? As we were coming to the Chapel this morning, we could hear the drums beating as you marched here. A famous American writer once asked: "Why should we be in such haste to succeed… if someone does not keep pace with everyone else, perhaps it is because he hears a different drummer."

The single-minded pursuit of success may bring with it all the trappings, and the flimsy, coveted symbols of achievement. But on the way to that kind of success, does anyone hear the beat of a different drummer? The drumbeat of Jesus of Nazareth, perhaps, saying something about gaining the whole world at the cost of yourself – or your self-respect. Let's not blame Zacchaeus too quickly.

And aren't all of us, like Zacchaeus tempted to suppress our past? I've just come back from South Africa. And I met two people there who'd been on the Truth and Reconciliation Commission. It was a gruelling experience, listening day after day to the horrors and evils that people had lived through.

Some of the people we met wondered if it had been the right way to proceed. Or if it had finished too soon. There is still a huge job to be done to help people on the fringes of the violence to come to terms with the past so that they can build a new South Africa that has integrity.

But the truth at the heart of the Commission was that history is not linear; it's cyclical. Unless we transform our past, it'll keep hitting us in the face in the future. And that goes for us as individuals as well as for communities. Cycles of fear, of bitterness, of deprivation, of poverty blight the lives of people and deny them life in all its fullness.

And aren't we all of us tempted by the very comfortable illusion that we live in a world where everything revolves around us, and others only matter if and when they do something for us?

I used to be a child psychologist. Very young children are just like that. They assume that everyone sees the world the way they do. A large part of growing up is learning to decentre; to look at the world through other people's eyes, literally and metaphorically. It can be difficult. And there are some areas in life where we never achieve the ability to break out of our own self-centredness.

Just like Zacchaeus up that sycamore tree. Separated from everyone else; only able to see everything from his perspective, and when that is blocked by the crowd, he climbs up a tree so that he can see more clearly.

But still with his eyes. And Jesus says to him: "Come down Zacchaeus. Today I'm going to be your guest." And to all of us, Jesus of Nazareth says: "I can break the shackles of your self-centredness: Today I want to be your guest".

Zacchaeus was a small man, and there's that smallness in each of us. And the Gospel is meant to draw us away from that smallness to the full stature of Christ. Who became man, in the sense that he became truly human, the one who fully realised and achieved what true humanity is all about.

Most of us want success and so achieve nothing
  Jesus made himself nothing and so achieved abiding
  success.
Most of us suppress our past and so pretend a future.
  Jesus was prepared to sacrifice his future to give us
  hope for our past.
Most of us are tempted to use people and lose all respect.
  Jesus won respect by being willing to let others make
  use of him.

Grow, says St Paul, to that maturity which is measured by nothing less than the full stature of Jesus Christ.

Sunday October 31st 2004, Sandhurst College

REACHING OUT

Luke 19: 1-10; Psalm 96

Let's think about the story of Zacchaeus.

He was a tax collector, his life summed up in that one
name, and shunned because of it.

Let us pray for those we too hold at arm's length,
The ones we think might contaminate our careful lives
Or might blow apart the identity we've crafted for
ourselves
The ones we just can't get through to
The ones society dismisses in a single, fearful name:
      paedophile, terrorist, trafficker, asylum seeker

Help us, Lord Jesus, to fill in the rest of the picture,
      To colour in the mother or son in the background
      To give shape to the swirling pain and tragedy of
      their lives
      And to discover where our own insecurity fits into it

        Lord, in your mercy,
        Hear our prayer.

Zacchaeus found himself on the edge of the crowd, in a
precarious position.

Let us pray for those who find themselves on the edge
      Geographically far from the main centres of
      population
      Socially excluded from facilities and support most

people are offered

Politically disenfranchised, seen as a problem for
others to sort out

On the edge of life, struggling with terminal illness

Help us, Lord Jesus, to be sensitive to the dignity of those
whose lives have taken a different path from our own
to know when they long to be part of our crowd
when they value their separate distinctiveness
and how together we can build a caring community

Lord, in your mercy
Hear our prayer.

Jesus reached over the heads of the crowd and drew
Zacchaeus to him.

Loving God
Today we pray for your church as we reach out in mission
in new places or in new ways
Protect us, we pray, from the arrogance of assuming we
are pioneers, that you have not gone before us.

Save us from the sin of self-sufficiency, of assuming we
can do without the insights and support of others or that
we live through our own strength alone.
Grant us, we pray, ears to hear the stories of others and
eloquence in telling our own stories of faith.
Sustain us, O Lord, through the sunburst of success, the
dark clouds of discouragement, with the candlepower of a
faith that is for sharing.

We ask it in the name of our searching, persistent Saviour, Jesus Christ. Amen

Wednesday, May 19th 2004, when the General Assembly discussed National Mission.

OF MOLES AND CUTTY STOOLS

If you visit Greyfriars Church in Edinburgh as a tourist, one of the items on display will be the Cutty Stool. It's a simple wooden piece, rather like the step you'd use in an old-fashioned library to get at the books on the top shelf, and it's crying out for a vase of flowers to be put on it. But, in its day, it was a serious instrument of torture. Anyone who'd fallen foul of the Kirk Session and was thought to have strayed from the path was displayed in shame in front of the congregation as a lesson to others.

Things have moved on, I'm glad to say, and in our less judgmental day the idea of the Cutty Stool is regarded with a sense of revulsion. The dominant thinking in the church emphasises forgiveness and reconciliation, rather than overt punishment. We are more aware of our own failings, more ready to acknowledge the flaws in our perception of God's justice, more conscious of the damage done to vulnerable people by this kind of treatment. It's in the pages of the tabloids that people are humiliated in public now.

But not in other parts of the world, where our Scottish legacy lives on. This autumn, I visited South Africa as Moderator. People were proud to show us the places that the missionaries had established and that they were still maintaining and they spoke about the schools and hospitals they had pioneered. We were feeling quite pleased with ourselves, in a reflected kind of way, until we took part in a service in a large church, full of several visiting congregations and recorded on video. At one point in the service, two girls were brought out to the front of the congregation. We were told that, at a meeting of the Kirk Session the previous evening, it had been decided to discipline them. They had strayed from the path and were to be suspended from church membership for an unspecified period. They were then replaced at the front by four other girls who had served their period of punishment and were to be readmitted to communion. It was hard for us to explain to the clergy just how appalled we were by this. They thought they were upholding the tradition they'd been given by our Scottish predecessors.

The reason I mention this today is because today is World Aids Day. Do we need to rehearse the figures? Or point out what a scourge it is in countries that are losing a whole tranche of their most able and active people, just when the convulsions of liberation were settling down into the hope of a stable future? And this year, the United Nations is highlighting the plight of women and AIDS. In most areas, an increasing proportion of people living with HIV/AIDS are women and girls. The sexual vulnerability of girls that was demonstrated in that church service in South Africa is particularly poignant in that context.

Where AIDS came from and what we should do about it is still a puzzle. But what is clear is that silence has caused untold deaths. The silence that is the natural response when we are afraid to admit to shortcomings in what is seen as correct moral behaviour. It has delayed treatment and methods of prevention that could have saved lives by the bucketful. A judgmental culture that was certain about right and wrong has done huge damage.

And the church has to take its share of the blame for that. With misplaced zeal, it has turned aspects of behaviour into measures of Christian faithfulness and pursued those who deviate from them with all the moral censure it can muster. In Scotland in the 17th century and in Southern Africa in the 21st.

Faith is a strange thing. As people of faith, our lives are shaped by belief in truths that are not open to falsification or rational test. We believe in God. We believe that God is love. We believe that Jesus Christ is the way, the truth and the life. These are powerful statements. But they're in a language spoken only by those who believe them. And in communicating with those who don't share the language, some have adopted the strategy, beloved of people in these islands, of simply shouting louder, of confusing belief in a truth with certainty about its consequences.

Truth and certainty aren't the same things. Certainty is a particular attitude to the truth, one which appears to be full of confidence but which is actually quite defensive and insecure. It carefully wraps the truth up into a little package, take it or leave it. But that kind of attitude misses things and is sterile, allowing for no growth of vision or of horizon.

The Israeli poet Yehuda Amichai writes about the sterility of certainty and of how it is doubts and loves that dig up the world like a mole.

The Christmas story is all about digging up the world like a mole. About jumbling up our assumptions about greatness and kingship and value. And it's the Magnificat that sums it all up best. Every mother-to-be hopes that her child will be special but Mary sings of the way her child, by the very circumstances of his birth, is going to change the whole world order just as God has begun to do by making her mother of his son: "He has scattered the proud in the imagination of their hearts. He has put down the mighty from their seats and exalted the humble and meek. He has filled the hungry with good things and the rich he has sent empty away."

Nothing neatly packaged about that world. The world of faith needs room to breathe, room for the Spirit to be active and for surprising things to happen. It's not a world where we tick the boxes of right behaviour, but one where we open ourselves to learning about the complexities of love and power and trust and dignity, the basic ingredients of human relationships which were at the heart of Jesus' teaching.

We often make a mess of dealing with moral issues. Too often, our thinking degenerates into a Puritanism that keeps up a front of respectability, a front that can hide the complexity of manipulative and abusive relationships. We need to dig up that world and let in some oxygen so that love and trust can flourish.

So let's end with a different picture of the Church and AIDS. This year, the Church of Scotland considered a report entitled *Better Late Than Never,* about HIV/AIDS and how the Church was supporting projects in Scotland and overseas. And let me tell you about one initiative I was able to see in South Africa.

In the Cape Town township of Guguletu, there is the J L Zwane Centre, a church supported by the University of Stellenbosch that is committed to facing up to AIDS. They talk about it. They sing about it. And at the heart of their ministry is the affirmation that "the Word was made flesh and dwelt among us". Among us, with all our faults and failings and our hopes.

We were introduced to a group of twelve young people, chosen as a result of a Pop Idol competition, who sang three songs for us. One was in English, based on the ABC guide of Abstain, Be faithful, use a Condom. The second was in Xhosa and was about the various myths about how to be cured of AIDS, myths that simply spread the illness further. And the third was from *Handel's Messiah*, "And the glory of the Lord shall be revealed. And all flesh shall see it together."

This Advent, as we prepare to listen to the story once more of God's boundless love for this world, may we see how it relates to the lives of those we shut up behind a wall of silent disapproval. And may we do something about it!

Wednesday December 1st 2004, The Crypt of the Houses of Parliament, Westminster.

BLESSINGS

Loving Lord
We pray for your blessing on the world you love
a world where people mourn
> loss of their loved ones and their livelihood in the
> tidal wave
> loss of innocence in young lives haunted by drugs
> and abuse
> loss of hope when illness is diagnosed
> loss of faith as they try to find you in complicated live

Lord, give them your blessing and grant them peace.

A world where people show mercy
> victims of crime who reach out to those who have
> hurt them
> wives and husbands whose love is unconditional
> governments that work for the cancellation of
> international debt
> prison staff who respect the dignity of those in their
> charge

Lord, give them your blessing and grant them peace.

A world where peacemakers struggle to see justice done
> in stair-head disputes
> in broken marriages
> in communities with a poisonous legacy of suspicion
> in Iraq where hope and fear struggle in voters' hearts
> this weekend

Lord, give them your blessing and grant them peace.

A brash world that does not value the strength of
    the quiet voice
    the meek stance
    the open, unassuming heart
    the disciplined life

Lord, give them your blessing and grant them peace.

Loving Jesus
you gave us a vision of what your Kingdom was like
    a small seed, spreading through the world
    salt that brings out the true flavour of life
    festivals at which the poor man is king
    mirrors in which the blind look at themselves
    and love looks back at them

We are your hands and feet in this world.
Grant that we may hold to the vision of your kingdom
and work for its coming.

We ask it in your name, Amen.

January 30th 2005, Musselburgh.

ENERGISING THE BODY OF CHRIST

Exodus 4: 10-16; Luke 22; 24-30

A new beginning. A milestone. Hurdles overcome. A breakthrough. Triumph. Recognition. You can use lots of different images to describe the impact of the decision to admit women to the priesthood ten years ago.

I used to be a developmental psychologist. That means that I tried to understand how children change, particularly how their thinking and language change in early childhood. Some change is gradual; children get more knowledgeable as their experience increases. Other change seems to come from nowhere; suddenly their way of looking at things switches over and a whole series of other changes in speech and understanding is triggered.

So too in public life. And in the church. Some changes are very visible. They've been hard fought for. They've become a *cause célèbre*. Others happen more quietly as people discover new ways of expressing their faith. And sometimes, the high profile cases lead to little changes that weren't expected. They generate a chain reaction of confidence and affirmation which suffuses the whole church. Little pockets of energy grow and make their presence felt and the whole body becomes very different.

So the impact of the visible breakthrough of women's ordination ten years ago was far greater than just an increase in the number and gender of priests; it also represented a coming of age for women's ministry in general.

So today, we celebrate the ground-breaking admission of women to the priesthood and we also celebrate the wider ministry that women offer the church.

Today, we celebrate new life: new life that, as always, was born of struggle and hurt and energy. New life that exposed the fallacy of the idea that things could not be different, that the shape and process of the church was fixed.

"But I say unto you…" How often do we hear Jesus say this? How often does he lay out the law and then throw it into doubt? Or allow it to grow and offer it a life-giving extension? Of course, it's natural for people to look for certainty in life and it's natural for the church to want to give it to them. But certainty is usually sterile when set in the kaleidoscopic world that we live in.

There's a wonderful Israeli poem I find myself quoting a lot, by Yehuda Amichai:

> From the place where you are right
> flowers will never grow
> in the Spring.
>
> The place where we are right
> is hard and trampled
> like a yard.
>
> But doubts and loves
> dig up the world
> like a mole, a plough.

And a whisper will be heard in the place
where the ruined
house once stood.

Yehuda Amichai, Selected Poetry

Today, we give thanks for those moles who were honest about their doubts and followed the promptings of love and challenged the square-bashing certainty that said that women couldn't or shouldn't have particular kinds of ministries. And we also pray for the courage to resist the temptations of stamping and hammering our own convictions on top of the new growth of other revelations.

Today, we celebrate new relationships. The story of the bickering disciples is devastating. It isn't only in poor taste. But, coming at the end of the account of the Last Supper, it emphasises just how little they understood about what was going on. And questions about status have kept coming up over the centuries to put blinkers on the church. And questions about status still cause problems.

About twenty years ago, we were on holiday in Normandy and we visited Lisieux. It's a little market town straight out of your old French grammar book. Every second man you meet looks as if he's someone's Oncle Henri, setting off on his *bicyclette* to the *boulangerie* for the *petit déjeuner.*

The town is on a hill and right at the top is a huge basilica, looking all the more enormous because of its prominent position. Inside, each chapel is gifted by a different country of Europe and the whole building is vast and splendid. Round it is a large coach park for the thousands of pilgrims that come to visit the site.

The irony is that it's in honour of St Theresa, a modest girl of a pious family who joined the Carmelite order and had made humility and simplicity her watchword. And the church has shown its approval of her life the best way it knows how, by building this enormous sanctuary, which, as far as I can see, completely nullifies the very humility and simplicity that she stood for.

This story has stayed with me as an illustration of the dilemma that any hierarchical system has in rewarding the delicate and subtle qualities that make life a pleasure. Or in acknowledging the special spiritual gifts that the church fosters and that, characteristically, women are encouraged to nurture. Status, hierarchy, position are crude instruments when placed next to compassion, or the power to heal. Yet compassion and healing are what the church is supposed to be concerned with.

The trouble with this passage in Luke is that it can't shake off the assumptions about greatness. It's a kind of *reductio ad absurdam*. Servants can't be leaders, leaders can't behave like children. It's not about turning the structure upside down, but about dissolving the structure. What needs to change is the very idea that one person should be greater than the other. Rather than concentrating on who has status, we should focus on serving each other and on serving God.

Can new generations of confident women sort this one out? Will they be less tolerant of competitiveness and power and more interested in nurturing notions of servanthood? I suspect your answer depends on the women you've met and the books you've read. Perhaps centuries of being out of the ecclesiastical limelight has indeed taught women the value of caring for each other and developing new kinds of relationships. Or perhaps not. We'll see! But the question is now on the agenda.

Today, we celebrate new voices. My bookshelves are full of books of prayers and sermons and poems by women written over the last decade or so. But this torrent of creativity built up slowly. "O my Lord, please send someone else." Moses' reaction is a very human one, especially for people whose voice is so often silenced. Yet soon the experience of being spoken for palls and we find our own voice.

> Prompt me, God
> When I speak,
> though it be you who speak
> through me, something is lost.

> Kneeling, R.S. Thomas, Collected Poems

However eloquent it might be, any exposition is only partial and it's filtered through the speaker's own experience and perspective. So we miss the completeness of the gospel unless we hear the voices of all groups, including women.

And their voices are distinctive. Women speak out of different bodies, from different places in society, with different life experiences. And they explore different styles and different expressions.

In time, these differences will be assimilated into the mainstream. Four weeks ago, the Archbishop of Canterbury preached a sermon to mark the tenth anniversary of the ordination of women. And it was an imagined monologue by Mary as she went to tell the disciples that she'd seen Jesus on Easter morning. At times Mary Magdalene sounded awfully like Rowan Williams, but the sermon was a tribute to the distinctive voices that women bring to worship and learning.

At one point, he has Mary say, "There'll be some of them who won't want to hear. That seems to belong to a world where things stay the same, where God has settled what he wants to say and left it there for us, carefully wrapped up. And I worry that that's a world where this morning doesn't happen."

Perhaps that's the really radical thing about women's ordination. It gives the lie to the kind of world where God wraps everything up and the resurrection doesn't happen. But we know it does and that there's no going back now.

June 12th 2004, St Mary's Episcopal Cathedral, Edinburgh to commemorate the 10th anniversary of the ordination of women in the Episcopal Church.

GIRLS' VOICES

Loving God
It is wonderful to have the freedom to sing our praises to
you

God of Creation
we think of the glorious world you have created
the mountains and valleys and beaches and cliffs
of Scotland
and of the countries we've come from
When we think of the beauty of your world
how can we keep from singing?

Generous God
we give you thanks for the gifts you have given us:
Intelligence to understand the way the world works
        and to make it more just and peaceful
Creative skill to make new and inspiring things
        and the sensitivity to appreciate them
Gifts of clear speech, graceful movement, the eyes of
artists and painters
        that add colour and interest to our lives
When we think of the generous gifts you have given us
how can we keep from singing?

God of love and friendship
we thank you for the love that is in our lives
the love of our family, which we often take for granted but
also rely on
the friendships that stretch our understanding of ourselves

and grow into something very precious
the care shown to us by strangers
who owe us nothing but are just good people
When we think of your love surrounding us through family,
friend and stranger
how can we keep from singing?

Loving, generous God
your greatest gift to us has been the faith that we live by
and the gift of you dear son, Jesus Christ
we are overwhelmed by how lucky we are
to know about the Christian Gospel
to be able to serve you
and to share our faith with other people
when we think of the joys of the Christian faith
how can we keep from singing?

Generous, loving, living God
We praise you, we thank you, we worship you, Amen

July 22nd, 2004, International Gathering of the Girls' Brigade in Glasgow.

LIVING AND LEARNING ON HOLY GROUND

Today is a day for celebrating the initiative and foresight of Bishop Elphinstone who founded this ancient university over 500 years ago and the generosity of its subsequent benefactors. It's a day for celebrating the achievements of the university over that time in discoveries made and lives transformed. And it's a day for asking God's blessing on the people who are this community and on the work that they do.

For five hundred years, students here have travelled on thrilling journeys in this place. Their eyes have been opened to new ways of looking at the world. Their minds have been stretched and buffeted and focused. They've searched with a new intensity and they've marvelled at what they had taken for granted. They've been changed for ever by the experience.

Lots of people looking in on a university think of it as a stuffy place – walls of books containing knowledge that has to be transferred from one memory to another. As if knowledge was a commodity rather than an adventurous process. And people often think that faith is also a commodity, a matter of listing propositions you believe, rather than the adventure of seeing the world through eyes that have been bathed in that faith. There are strong parallels between the intellectual and the spiritual journey. As you move from one academic discipline to another, you ask different questions, you look for different things, you see dimensions to life that were previously hidden. As you do in the journey of faith.

I had to learn about how disciplines inhabit different worlds in my first year at university. I found myself having to do a course in physics, having done no science at school. But I had overdosed on mathematics. And I assumed the two subjects were similar. Not so. I puzzled over why it was OK to draw a conclusion from a few observations in the physics class while, for a mathematician, you have to prove a formula in the general case before you can make any claims. The scientific method had to be discovered and in the process the limits of its authority were exposed.

In later years, I tended to gravitate to the boundaries of disciplines. My research was in psycholinguistics, and I had to keep clear in my mind the questions asked by the psychologists and those asked by the linguists and not judge the one by the standards and methods of the other. In church and society work, you have to translate from the language and concerns of the politician to those of the theologian. And in the Centre for Theology and Public Issues, in the University of Edinburgh, we facilitate conversations between academics, practitioners, policy makers and those affected by policy. Same theme, same endlessly fascinating world, different ways of knowing.

But not all ways of knowing have the same value in the Christian faith. One of the tussles in the gospels is that between the dominant perspective of the lawyer, shorn of the particularity of individual human experience but aligned with the powerful and successful, and the world as it is seen by the weak and the poor, the perspective that Jesus liberated from the margins, reminding us all that for God it's justice for the poor that matters. At the heart of his ministry, he placed the outcast, the oppressed, the needy and claimed their Jubilee right to be heard and released. The eyes of faith look out compassionate on the world.

And these eyes are trained and lubricated by parable and metaphor, just as academic minds are mediated by models and data. In the church we tell stories and paint pictures; mathematicians draw diagrams; psychologists build theoretical models.

I once had a colleague who studied the history of theories of mental process and traced how these theories reflected the dominant machines of the time. I can't remember all the details now but we certainly had the hydraulic model of mind at the apex of the age of the great Victorian municipal engineering works. And by the 70s when I knew about these things, the mind was definitely a computer, with hardware and software, programmes and storage devices. Pictures help to explain things, which is why we have these powerful parables of the kingdom in the gospels. The kingdom of heaven is like a mustard seed. Or like yeast. Or like a field sown with good seed and bad. Like a treasure hidden in a field. Like a pearl of great price. But they're not static illustrations. They have within them movement and yearning and growth. They carry the believer on, haunt your mind and speak to you in moments of uncertainty and pain. Listen to the parables of the treasure hidden in a field and of the pearl of great value, the pearl that is at the heart of the anthem* specially composed for today's service.

> The kingdom of heaven is like treasure hidden in a field,
> which someone found and hid; then in his joy he goes and
> sells all that he has and buys that field.

> Matthew 13: 44

> Again, the kingdom of heaven is like a merchant in search
> of fine pearls; on finding one pearl of great value, he went
> and sold all that he had and bought it.

> Matthew 13: 46

These parables illustrate beautifully the passion of the search after truth, be it intellectual or spiritual. And the thrill of its discovery. I love the story of the research scientist who had just made a significant breakthrough, hugging himself and saying, "I know something no-one else knows, and they're not going to know it until I tell them". You can imagine him savouring the moment, delaying the announcement of what he'd found, to enjoy the pleasure of having found what he was looking for.

We sell science short by insisting on a clinical rationality in its telling. The search for truth has always been an adventure, stumbling along, not in darkness but in a twilight pierced by glimpses of its presence, as R S Thomas notes. And he picks up the field and the pearl in a poem about revelation, be it spiritual or scientific:

> I have seen the sun break through
> to illuminate a small field
> for a while, and gone my way
> and forgotten it. But that was the pearl
> of great price, the one field that had
> the treasure in it. I realise now
> that I must give all that I have
> to possess it.

The language of discovery and the language of faith are often impoverished because we rush on unimaginatively to a statement of conclusions. For a long time I bought into the idea that the Bible was a blueprint for action, a collection of pat questions and answers. But no; it's an invitation to keep rediscovering the meaning of God's love in the particularity of our lives. God is ahead of us, doing a new thing, surprising us.

The poem continues:

> Life is not hurrying
> on to a receding future, nor hankering after
> an imagined past. It is the turning
> aside like Moses to the miracle
> of the lit bush, to a brightness
> that seemed as transitory as your youth
> once but is the eternity that awaits you.

The Bright Field, RS Thomas, Collected Poems

Miracles. One of the great gifts of a scientific training is learning how miraculous the every day is. Things we take for granted astound us by their intricacy once we try to understand them. The miracle of a mother communicating with her baby. The mystery of how a string quartet goes beyond playing notes to making music. The impossibility of learning to speak your first language. These are from my own background but you'll have your own examples.

And the miraculous burning bush brings us back home. To here. To holy ground. To a place where God is.

In my tradition we don't set much store by particular holy places. To buildings that have been blessed and set aside for holy purposes. But we do care about the places where God is to be found. And these are places of pain and of joy.

For me this is holy ground. The last time I was in this chapel was at the funeral of our niece. She was a student at this university and she died at the age of 21 from a virus that affected her heart. It was a time for hugging and for crying. For letting familiar words settle and heal. It brought us right to the heart of this university, to the caring love of the community, the hope and vitality of young lives and the mysteries of faith and of scientific enquiry. It was a precious, painful moment.

For five hundred years, this has been holy ground, a place of intense searching, passionate discovery, love and awe and wonder. Journeys of faith and enquiry have shadowed each other, held together in God's caring love. The searching and the love will continue and we ask God's blessing on these journeys.

* The words were adapted by Scott Styles from the Latin of the Papal Bull granted by Pope Alexander VI in 1495, establishing the University of Aberdeen. "Amongst the various blessings which mortal man is able to obtain by the gift of God, it is reckoned not among the least, that earnest study may win the pearl of knowledge. Knowledge shows the heart of the living God, it reveals life's secrets, and leads to a clear understanding of the secrets of the universe, and raises to eminence those born in low estate. O Lord, our God and King, our Saviour dear, who bled and died for us, O Lord..."

Sunday February 13th, 2005, King's College Chapel, Aberdeen, at the University of Aberdeen's Founder's Day Service.

LISTENING AND LEARNING
1 Corinthians 13: 8-13; Psalm 8

Lord Jesus,
We listen to the voices of children
> tentative
> refreshing in their uncluttered vision
> incomplete, yet perceptive
> open in their loves and in their hostility

We hear in them our own unvarnished instincts and
passions
Lord Jesus, you made space for little children at the heart
of your Kingdom.
Grant that we may mature in the ambit of your love.

We listen to the voices of the poor
> resilient
> proud
> resigned
> betrayed

We hear in their struggle our neglect of them and the
failure of our love towards you.
Lord God, your insistent care for the poor reverberates
down the years.
Bind us together and so enrich us all.

We listen to the voices of specialists,
> probing the complexity of today's world
> struggling to translate their language into ours
> challenging received wisdom and settled behaviour

We hear risk and promise, caution and censure.
Creator God, you have set us in a world of majesty and
intricacy.
Give us a right respect for its mystery and a fair
celebration of its abundance.

We listen to the voices of the powerful
    commanding
    cajoling
    carving out paths for others to follow.
We hear our own willingness to be led and the temptations
and attractions of high office.
God of power and might, you took the form of a servant.
Remind us of the looking glass world that we aspire to,
where prisoners go free, the
blind see and the oppressed find release.

We listen to the voices of our neighbours
    young,
    poor,
    knowledgeable,
    powerful
We hear there the partial echoes of the world you can
hear, the world you love.
Grant us the voice today to speak of that love, in the name
of our great teacher, guide and Lord, Jesus Christ our
Lord. Amen

*Tuesday May 18th, the General Assembly discussion on Church and
Society.*

ADVENTUROUS DREAMS

Today, it's Founder's Day and we're thinking about George Watson, the person who founded this school more than 250 years ago. He was a merchant, who made lots of money and left it so that children in Edinburgh could have a good education. Life had obviously been good to him and he must have wanted to show his thanks for all that. And today, it's our turn to thank him for giving us the chance to go to school here.

Thinking back over 250 years. It's hard to think ourselves into that time. So much was different. Not just how we travel. Watson would have had to sail overseas by boat, not jump on an Easyjet plane and complain because the take-off had been delayed by an hour. Not just because of the kinds of things he would have been selling. But because they were different people, with different ways of thinking, different ideas about how society worked. So it's hard to think back over 250 years.

But it's easier than thinking forward 250 years. Or even 25 years. It's not just a question of not knowing what might happen. You don't know how you're going to change. What kind of a person you're going to be.

When I was at school, I could never have thought ahead to what I'm doing now. I never imagined that I'd be speaking to you now, as Moderator of the General Assembly of the Church of Scotland. When I was at school, women were not allowed to be ministers, or even elders in the church, so it just never entered my head. Even all those years when I sat in this hall watching my children play their violin or their trombone in a concert, it never occurred to me that this would happen.

In fact, one phrase that keeps coming into my mind, and my

conversation this year is "Who'd have thought it?" Lots of people have been in touch with me from my past and I've had lots of conversations along the lines of "Remember when we were doing our psychology practicals, training pigeons to peck at green lights? Who'd have thought then that you'd be Moderator one day?" Or, "Remember when we were rehearsing *Oklahoma* for the school musical? Who'd have thought then that you'd be speaking at Founder's Day one day?" And so on. I can certainly guarantee that, when I was in third year and the Moderator came to visit the school – it was Professor James S Stewart, a famous man and a great hero of my mother - it would never have entered my head or anyone else's to think that I'd be here today in his shoes, if not in his silver buckles and lace jabot.

I enjoyed school. And the subject I liked best was mathematics. I loved watching all the patterns forming and different shapes emerging. And it was great when I worked out a difficult problem.

When I left school, I thought I wanted to be an actuary. They're people who work in insurance companies and earn lots of money. But I then got a summer job in an insurance office and that soon put paid to that idea. But others took its place and I followed my maths degree with one in psychology and did research into how children learn language. When my own children were born, I left my job in Edinburgh University and got involved in work on how the church makes comments on political developments. That was tremendously exciting and it meant that I met lots of fascinating people and it stretched me in all kinds of ways.

And now I'm Moderator. It's only for one year, but you pack a tremendous amount of interesting experiences into it. Basically, I represent the Church of Scotland at various events and make visits to places the Church is interested in and cares about. In the last month, amongst many other things, I attended the Summit on Sectarianism, visited an oil platform, where they're planning to set up an off-shore wind farm, had dinner with the Speaker of the House of Commons and several MPs, preached at Founders Day services in both Aberdeen and St Andrew's Universities, spoke to a meeting of Christians and Jews in Glasgow, and tomorrow we're off to Toronto, where I'll preach at an anniversary service and give a lecture in a University College. And so on.

So that's a few of the adventures I've had in my life. And if you're reading an adventure story, you really want just to get on to the next page and not spoil the fun by looking ahead to how it's going to turn out. So I hope that, whether or not you've made up your mind about what you want to do with your life, it'll turn out to be exciting and more of an adventure than you expect.

But some people want to look ahead, or need to look ahead, to plan what to do with their lives, to dream about what might be possible, or what might happen to them. Some have decided exactly the kind of life they want, even if it's not very exciting, not maybe as interesting as it could be if they had allowed things to happen more, and they put out a tremendous amount of energy into making sure it will happen. You know the kind of person. There's always someone in the Sixth Year's Year Book who's "most likely" to have their life mapped out well in advance.

Other people dream of the impossible. They dream that they'll discover the cure for a terrible illness, or run a huge international company that is bigger than Microsoft, or go on Big Brother, or be a famous singer. And some of them don't just dream about it, they work at it until it happens. They're ambitious; they drive their dream forward until they get there.

But what's an impossible dream to some people is what the rest of us take for granted. Zechariah dreamed of old men and women sitting outside, and children playing in the streets. Or think of the wee girl in the poem that was read to us. All she dreamed about was a bath, a clean sheet, a pillow and a warm blanket. She lived in a tin shack with a dusty mud floor and she felt she was dreaming of the impossible. She wanted to get this dream back but didn't know how to.

I met children like her when I was in South Africa this autumn. As you know, in the big cities in South Africa, there are areas full of people who surge in from the country to find work and set up poor houses, made out of sheets of corrugated iron or bits of container trucks, and they grow up in these houses. Thousands of people live in these townships and some of the townships have been going for over a hundred years. But it's tough. We visited a nursery school near Cape Town. It was crowded with wee children who were playing, but had hardly any toys to play with. When we were there, it was a sunny day and dry, but the school had a mud floor and was built over the drains so when it got wet, the school flooded. The local church was getting money together to build a new school for them.

That makes people angry. And one person we met had tried to do something about it. His name was Tsepho Ndlovu. He lived in Soweto, a famous township in Johannesburg. He was born in 1961, and, as a schoolboy, he'd been active in politics. He was Chair of the School Debating Society and sometimes he'd tell his parents he was going to study but he'd go to political meetings instead. He and his friends got very angry about the unfair way that the country was run. They weren't allowed to be taught in their own language, which made things even more difficult for children who already had a hard time getting any qualifications because they were so poor. So one day, in 1976, when he was fifteen, they decided that they would go on a march to the building of the education authority to complain. There were thousands of them and they planned the march very carefully. But someone told the police, and they were waiting for them.

The first student they shot was Hector Petersen, a boy of thirteen. There's a famous photo of him being carried away from the tragedy. By the end of that day, 23 students had been killed. Two weeks later, the Security Services ransacked Tsepho's house looking for evidence and he was arrested for taking part in the march. He had a terrible time and the charges were eventually withdrawn and he was sent to another part of South Africa.

He is now a businessman employing 150 people making sachets and food cartons. He's a church elder. His wife is in education, writing syllabuses for maths and science. He's a good friend of Nelson Mandela, the man who became President of South Africa, once the unfair laws of apartheid were changed. So his dream has come true, but only after a long struggle.

Sometimes these dreams are all washed away and you are left with having to decide what the really important things are in life.

In January, I was booked to go to India anyway, so when the tsunami struck, we decided to visit Sri Lanka as well. It was a terrible tragedy. We met people who had narrowly escaped with their lives and others who had lost family in the wave. One person who had been killed was a violin teacher in Colombo and her death had touched the lives of lots of people. We met Kirk, who is about eight. He'd only been playing his violin for three months but he played two tunes for us. One was Coulter's Candy, because they'd been learning tunes from different countries and had just done Scotland. The other was a tune he'd composed in memory of his teacher. It was a very special moment.

People in the fishing villages had lost everything. They'd lost their houses. They'd lost their fishing boats and their nets. They'd lost all the things that meant something special to them, presents from people who were important to them, things they'd saved up for. One wee boy was asked what he'd lost. "I've lost my friends" he said. When it comes to the bit, it's the other people that matter. Making friends, learning from them and caring for them, is one of the most important things you'll do in life. And it starts in school. You never know when you're going to come across someone you were at school with. And when you do, you'll find that there's a bond there that is very special. And that's possible because George Watson left his money to found this school 264 years ago. It's something worth saying thank you for.

March 4th, 2005, George Watson's College Founder's Day Service.

THY KINGDOM COME

Lord Jesus
You came among us to lead us to your Kingdom
Inspire us with a vision of that kingdom
As we serve and nurture each other here

Your Kingdom is like a mustard seed
Small and fragile but growing into a big tree
Lord Jesus
It's easy to get discouraged when we think of the
problems around us
Bless the small steps we take
To heal broken lives and to nurture hope
And grant that their effects will ripple through our
community.

In your Kingdom the usual expectations are turned upside
down.
The first are last and child-like qualities are admired
Lord Jesus
It's easy to admire people who are strong and successful
and to want to be like them
Help us to learn from those who are weak and who don't
seem to have much to offer.
Give us patience and generosity
As we make space in our community for everyone.

In your Kingdom justice is the starting point for generosity
and mercy.
Lord Jesus

It's easy to think of ourselves and our own problems all
the time
Teach us to look beyond our own needs and rights
To the needs and rights of the person next door
Or in the next street
Or in another country
Grant us the imagination to stand in their shoes
And the generosity to help them first

In your Kingdom, everyone has some talent, something to
offer the rest of us
Lord Jesus
It's easy to dismiss people who are slow or old or
hampered by an obvious disability
Help us to see beyond their difficulties
To the other gifts they have and the other skills they can
contribute to our community

Lord Jesus
You told your friends not to be afraid
And promised your Kingdom to a little group of people just
like us
Not very reliable
Not very faithful
Not very courageous
As we follow you on the way to your Kingdom
Grant that we may be propelled along by your love. Amen

November 21st, 2004, Paisley.

FOR AN ANNIVERSARY

"This is the day that the Lord has made. We will rejoice and be glad in it"

Today is a day for rejoicing for myself and Jo, my husband, because you have invited us to share this celebration with you. That's a great privilege and may I thank you for making this visit possible for us. We were given a tremendous welcome last night at the special 175th anniversary dinner and I had a chance to hear something of the history of this congregation from Brian Stewart's vigorous account of it, with special emphasis on the strong women of this place. And I heard several similarities between your story and that of our own congregation in Edinburgh, at Greyfriars, also a city centre church, also a historic building, also a church with a special ministry to the homeless. So we feel at home with you.

At the start of my year as Moderator, I was puzzled by why people were so keen to ask me to share in their anniversary celebrations. Such occasions are, at first blush, very private affairs. But that is to neglect the insight that we are all part of the one body and if one part celebrates, so does the whole. So my first message is to say, on behalf of the General Assembly of the Church of Scotland, and by extension, of the rest of the Church, Congratulations and every blessing for the future. We are all celebrating with you.

An anniversary is like a hinge. You both look forward and look backwards. So today we're celebrating the faith of our predecessors, and the promise of the future and God's nurturing presence throughout. We're giving thanks for all the mini miracles that these walls have witnessed throughout their history; vows of baptism and marriage exchanged and honoured; times of mourning and loss recognised; moments of healing gratefully acknowledged. And we're looking ahead, committing ourselves afresh to being the church in this part of the world.

Today, we are celebrating a particular story, the story of what makes this congregation different from the one next door. In a shrinking, globalised world, let us celebrate the particularity of this place.

One way of telling the story of this congregation is to give its public history. Its origins; the dates of the dedication of the building; the names of its ministers; the plans for the building; the sources of its furnishings.

That kind of story is the one that can be documented. It's the story that the wider church uses, to ensure that the congregation is in good health, to make decisions about how the Church's resources overall should be distributed. It covers the kind of information the Presbytery asks for in order to decide whether you can get permission to call a new minister. It's the key that allows the church to make sure that its resources are being well used and distributed.

And that process makes assumptions about what matters in congregational life and the overall shape it should take. Often, it requires congregations to fit a mould that doesn't reflect the ministry that they believe is needed in their setting. In any case, it doesn't go to the heart of the matter, to how God is worshipped in this place and how Christian faith is nurtured here.

We often puzzle over what makes for a faithful, vibrant congregation and it's strangely reassuring to discover that this question was being asked by Micah all these centuries ago, eight hundred years before

Christ. Faced with the amazing record of God's protection and faithfulness throughout history, the believer asks what kind of sacrifice, what kind of ritual cult can possibly satisfy such a powerful God. And the suggestions get more and more fanciful: calves, thousands of rams, tens of thousands of rivers of oil, even the sacrifice of his child. He's answering his own question. You can't match God's goodness with action and ritual: it's a completely different kind of relationship from the tit for tat transactions that we're familiar with in daily life. But it does call for a response. And that response is simple: to do justice, to love kindness and to walk humbly with your God.

Over the years, people in this congregation will have done that and it's the memory and the record of their faithfulness and love that has created the real congregation here. It's that that makes this congregation special. And it's that that we are celebrating today.

Today is also a special Sunday, because it's Mothering Sunday, the day when we celebrate the idea of the church as our mother. So, let us celebrate today the wider church family of which we are a part.

It's easy to get sentimental about mothers and it's easy to get sentimental about the church too. But those of us who are mothers know the temptations to be anything but lovable. The temptation to dominate, to manipulate, to play the trump card of "Because I say so."

And these are temptations that are not unknown to the church as well. The fuzzy line between theological wisdom and social control is one which has been fudged on many occasions.

But mothers can do amazing things. Like the mother who threw herself in front of her daughter, when a gunman attacked her and her family, in a modern image of sacrifice. The same kind of sacrifice that is attributed to the pelican, which is reputed to peck at its breast and feed its young with its own blood. In the National War Memorial of Scotland, which records all those in the services who were killed during the Great Wars, and those since, there is a pelican over the door, representing that fabled act of sacrifice.

And, like the pelican, Mother-Church is at her best when at her most sacrificial.

It can be a vulnerable role being a mother. When Jesus' mother was at her most vulnerable, watching her son die, he said to his closest friend, "Son, behold your mother" and to his mother, "Mother, behold your son". And in this, Christ gave us all responsibility for each other. So Mother Church should be a place where those who don't know any family affection can find it. And those who have no friends can find friends.

Any congregation is strongly identified with its church building, so part of today's celebrations has to do with this building. And so we give thanks for the architects, for the masons, for the embroiderers, the stained glass artists. For the musicians who've filled it with glorious sound, the flower arrangers, the cleaners. We give thanks for the special rites of passage hallowed in this place. For public acts of commemoration and memories too precious to be shared.

We love our church buildings. And understandably so. Great care has gone into making them beautiful, and our churches have always been places that have allowed people to express their faith in artistic, pleasing ways, through commissions and bequests.

They are changing. Much of the traditional architecture and furnishings are constraining in ways that are not helpful, and probably never have been. Our Committee on Artistic Matters has a front row seat in monitoring these changes and, by and large, they welcome the thoughtfulness that churches are expending in making their buildings more appropriate to the requirements of worship.

But they warn against the trend to make the church more comfy, more domesticated. There comes a point where these changes reflect a more fundamental change in the perceived purpose of the building, where people start thinking of the church as "a home for the people of God" rather than the "house of God" as it's usually described. And that often goes along with thinking of the church as ministering only to the congregation, rather than offering worship that is public and ministry that is open to the needs of the wider community. It can lead to a chumminess that is off-putting to people who're not part of the club. And our gospel reading is a warning to us not to become too much of a club.

It's a favourite story, the story of Zacchaeus. He was the little man that was so unpopular that nobody would make room for him so that he could see Jesus walk by. People thought of him as a collaborator with the occupying force, probably on the make, nobody's friend. He was someone who would contaminate the lives of decent people. He was best kept at arms length.

Yet it was with Zacchaeus that Jesus chose to spend the night. Not with the respectable pillars of society. Jesus kept doing these unexpected things, embarrassing his friends by the company he kept, going out of his way to look for society's rejects. He frequented the temple, of course, but he didn't limit himself to doing what other people thought he should do or going where they thought he should go.

So, if our churches are to be the house of God, they need to be places where we find the people God seeks out. A sanctuary and a shrine for all people, a place of strength for the weak, of refuge for the troubled where the hospitality of God's love radiates so that all can share it.

And, if that's what our church is like, it will be a place from which people go out, strengthened to do God's will in the world he loves. There's a lot of talk these days in the Church of Scotland about becoming a *Church without Walls*, a church that broadens its horizons and follows Christ out into the lives of people wherever they are. A church made up of people who do justice, wherever injustice is found, who love kindness and find it in lives scarred by violence and who walk humbly with their God.

Like every day, today's a day for looking forward. For building on the foundations laid by the people who have worshipped here for many years. For trusting that our God is a God who makes things new. For having confidence in the good news of Jesus Christ. For launching out to meet him in the world that he loves and following where he leads. It's an exciting time and I wish God's blessing on your onward journey!

March 6th, 2005, St Andrew's, Toronto.

CELEBRATING CHURCH LIFE

2 Corinthians 4: 1-12

Light of God
Flood the earth with your power
Invade our hearts and dwell within us

God of life and of truth
We come together this evening from different corners of
the world
    Brazil and Burma
    Budapest and Geneva
    inner cities and leafy suburbs
    rolling farmland and island croft
from different walks of life
    in council offices
    in general hospitals
    in shopping centres
    in schools and nursing homes
filtering your message through different traditions and
different personalities
    building strong communities
    creating things of beauty to your glory
    telling the story of your redeeming love
Yet it is you who have formed us all
you who have claimed us
you whose light burns within us
you whose power sustains us

Protect us, we pray, from the arrogance of self-sufficiency,
    thinking we don't need each other,
      believing we succeed through our own strength

promoting our own skills of presentation rather than
the truth of your gospel of love
And grant that your light will shine brightly in our lives.

Inscrutable God,
we know what fragile carriers of your message we are
we forget that you love us
we get distracted by esoteric arguments
we fight among ourselves
and we give up too easily

Yet it is *us* you have entrusted with the treasure of your
living power
the power to disturb, to heal, to refine our world, your
world
May we cherish our calling as your children
and grant that your power will be released through our
lives

Healing God
the clay jar that holds your treasure has already been
shattered
your church bears the marks of vicious conflict and it
struggles to find integrity in its life and worship
yet its resilience in the face of division and neglect is
remarkable
and your light still burns in its several parts
gather together the pieces of your church
that we may see more easily the shape of your love
and celebrate its reconciling power
in our lives and in the world

We ask this in the name of your Son, our physician and Lord, Jesus Christ. Amen

Sunday May 16th, when the General Assembly received overseas visitors and delegates from other churches.

REFRESHMENT AND HOLIDAYS

Amos 8: 1-12; Luke 10: 38-42.

This poem is called *Lewis in Summer*. But, if you go to the far side of this island, it could just as well be called *Iona in Summer*. It's by Derick Thomson, originally in Gaelic. And it goes like this:

> The atmosphere clear and transparent
> As though the veil had been rent
> And the Creator were sitting in full view of His people
> Eating potatoes and herring,
> With no man to whom he can say grace
> Probably, there's no other sky in the world
> That makes it so easy for people
> To look in on eternity;
> You don't need philosophy
> Where you can make do with binoculars

> Derick Thomson, Plundering the Harp:
> Collected Poems 1940-1980

Painters, writers, musicians have all tried to express the peculiar spiritual quality of the West Highland and Hebridean experience. That apparently effortless connection with the infinite that overcomes you. Or the moment when the beauty around you expands your soul till it hurts. And the peace that heals and slows and uplifts.

I like Thomson's picture of God being caught out, eating his tatties and herring, without saying grace because there's no-one he can say it to. He's a genial, domestic, comfortable God of the kind you might meet on a lazy summer's evening, a God you can relax with, one who will listen and encourage you and affirm you. The kind of God we want to believe in. But you can imagine that the Highlander's direct line to heaven on a stormy winter's night will reveal a very different picture: an angry God, a powerful God, possibly a vengeful God, the kind of God we assume we can relegate to the pages of the Old Testament.

And so we get a sense of how important setting can be in shaping our understanding of the faith. You read the Bible very differently when sitting on a Scottish island from the way in which you read it in the middle of London. Perhaps we also see how important philosophy, or theology, is to lessen the impact, or at least to broaden the context, of the God we see with our binoculars.

I expect we all have different reasons for being on Iona today. But many of us will be here hoping that a spell on Iona will knit up the ravelled sleeve of a busy year of work or responsibility. Getting away from it, a bit of peace and quiet, a change of perspective, slowing down, time to retreat and reflect – we all need it.

Taking time out has many benefits. A few weeks ago, I visited the Lodging House Mission in Glasgow. They provide meals and other services for people who are homeless. And one of their most prized possessions is a minibus. Every so often, they take a trip to Balloch and go hill walking round Loch Lomond. And they get the fresh air and the exercise that's at a premium in the city. But for many of them, whose lives are on hold and damaged by drugs, it's a chance to fill the day with healthy activity, to sense the achievement of getting to the top of a hill. And relationships with the staff take on a new colour and stories are told and confidences are shared and barriers broken down.

I expect that something similar happens when young folk come to Camas and I'm looking forward to visiting there tomorrow and hearing about the plans for expansion. Years ago, one of my friends brought a group of children to the Youth Camp here from one of the poorest housing estates in Edinburgh. Quite apart from the effect it had on the children, it took her a long time to come to terms with what she learned as she watched them take physical risks and probe social boundaries and come back the stronger. So there's more to holidays than rest and a long lie. It's a chance for spiritual growth and healing and energising.

One of the things I've been doing is going round various Church Assemblies. And one of the issues that is coming up in the assemblies I've been at is the ministry of healing and its relationship to spirituality. It's a live issue and a point of growth in the church. Even the Scottish Executive is recognising that there is a spiritual dimension to healing in its review of chaplaincy, which involves hospitals setting up a Department of Religious and Spiritual Healthcare.

Some churches have, in their own way, always given this a high priority. Ten days ago, a group of people from the St Andrews and Edinburgh Archdiocese set off to Lourdes. They spoke of the support they found in each other's company, the commitment to regular mass when there and the value of considering their work worries in a new light. It's no wonder that this tradition of a healing pilgrimage is so enduring. But the Reformed tradition has tended to neglect the quiet, contemplative life, or even a spot of contemplation in an active one.

A month ago, I was in Zürich, where, this summer, they're celebrating the 500th anniversary of the birth of Heinrich Bullinger. He was an important Reformer. He's not as well known as Zwingli, who was the first leader of the Reformation in Zürich and whose work he consolidated. But he was still a significant figure and this anniversary is an opportunity to mount exhibitions and celebrations about the Reformation there and they're well worth visiting, if you get the chance.

One of the snippets of information I picked up there was that Bullinger and the Reformers of his day reduced the number of holidays in Zürich from 120 to 63, just over half, retaining only Sundays and major festivals. Not surprisingly, this was good for business, resulting in greater productivity, more savings and a stronger economy. And so the seeds were sown of the Protestant work ethic; and the saints of the 16th century in Zürich gave way to the gnomes of the 20th.

This came to mind when I was reading the passage in Amos. It sets out with merciless energy and vibrant imagery the danger of a completely materialist society, where only the pursuit of wealth and the health of the economy matter. Where people become simply economic units and integrity is lost. Corruption sets in. They make the ephah small and the shekel great, and practise deceit with false balances. Buying the poor for silver and the needy for a pair of sandals and selling the sweepings of the wheat. A deeply inhuman society. I don't know whether Bullinger's stewardship was like this or not, and I understand that Calvin set out special rules in Geneva to protect the poor. But it lays out the dangers we need to avoid. Christian Aid and the Church of England have just published a booklet outlining the theological background to the Trade Justice campaign, which argues that our present system of trade is unjust and idolatrous, and it leans heavily on this passage in Amos.

Interestingly, Amos locates part of the warning signs of an unjust economic system in an impatience with the holidays, Holy Days, feast days, that give shape to the pace of life and rest to those who do the work. "When will the New Moon be over so that we may sell grain; and the Sabbath so that we may offer wheat for sale?" An impatience that leads to neglect and loss of the spiritual dimension to life – a famine of hearing the words of the Lord. And, as with any famine, people then recognise their need, running to and fro, seeking the word of the Lord, but not finding it.

Is this what had happened to Martha? Luke draws attention, not just to her hard work, but to her being distracted, lacking focus, swamped by her responsibilities, losing sight of the important priorities in life. And she's contrasted with the single-minded Mary. It's a tantalising vignette of domestic tensions, in many ways very perceptively drawn.

Like many women, I warm to Martha. It's easy to see her as someone who wanted to do her best for the guest we're told that she'd welcomed into her house, as well as wanting to enjoy his company and listen to him. Someone had to get the room ready and make the supper and if the jobs had been shared out, then maybe all three could have enjoyed the visit. Her plea for help was met with that familiar response from those who don't understand what goes on behind the scenes – not, "We'll help", but "It's not important! Stop worrying!"

However we understand the story, I'm sure it's more subtle than just a competition between a life of action and a life of contemplation. Between work and spiritual health. Because being human means holding both together. And being Christian involves seeing how each interpenetrates the other. And the Iona Community has been most assiduous in developing that relationship.

It's a particular privilege to spend time on Iona. We're all very lucky. There's the calming effect of remoteness here, being on an island off an island off the mainland of an island. Yet it's not isolation. At every turn, the opportunity is given for plugging in to the heartbeat of the world:

• For making imaginative contact with the lives of people
on the other side of the globe or in our own frenetic
cities.

- For taking time to reflect prayerfully on issues of justice and peace.

- For directing our minds and energies towards new ways of living and to uncovering the values that will sustain that.

- For understanding afresh the fundamental, healing reality of Christ's incarnation, that takes the mystery and liberation and power of the divine and places it in ordinary people and makes of them extraordinary lives.

And at the heart of the mystery is a simple meal. A meal shared with friends like Martha and Mary. A meal that takes the staples of bread and wine, that someone has worked to make, and makes them special as Christ's body and blood. And that makes us whole.

18th July 2004, Iona Abbey.

GOD BE IN MY HEAD

God be in my head, and in my understanding.

Almighty God,
You have set us in a world of majesty and intricacy
with minds that want to know why things happen,
that try to control the way things work,
that are stretched by the discoveries and the questions of
the great laboratory that is your world
We give thanks for the richness of your wonderful creation
and for the ingenuity that has made our lives healthier,
safer and better connected with each other.

Grant to our scientists humility,
to the commercial world generosity
and to ourselves sensitivity
as we advance our knowledge of your world.

God be in mine eyes, and in my looking.

Loving God,
we see through a glass darkly,
our perceptions shaped by our experience
our interpretations influenced by forces that are often
hidden from us.

Remind us of our calling as your children
and grant that we may look at the world through your eyes
the eyes of compassion for the weak and of care for those
who suffer

God be in my mouth, and in my speaking.

God of friend and family
our lives are shaped round relationships with others
and the oil that lubricates these relationships is
communication
we pray for those for whom speaking is difficult
little children struggling to be understood
old friends walking on eggshells round a delicate misun-
derstanding
preachers and politicians trying to explain and persuade
about matters of great importance
and for ourselves as we judge when to speak and when to
keep quiet

grant that all may use words informed by your truth and
uttered in love

God be in my heart, and in my thinking.

Almighty God
unto whom all hearts are open
all desires known
and from whom no secrets are hidden
we often struggle with what motivates us
with who the real me is
with where the other person is coming from

Teach us to trust you
to guide our lives
so that we deal honestly with each other
and build communities of love and integrity

God be at my end, and at my departing.

Eternal God,
we are especially conscious this evening of all those
whose ministry in this valley
has laid the foundations of the church we know today

Grant that we may be true to their memory
by showing courage in addressing the needs of our day
openness to the gifts of others
and generosity in sharing the good news of your love
that your Kingdom may come close
in our lives and in this community.

This we ask in the name of our Lord and Saviour,
Jesus Christ. Amen

Sunday June 20th 2004 Broughton.

LOVE WITHOUT 'IFS' OR 'BUTS'

Deuteronomy 30: 15-20; Luke 14: 25-33

It's a great privilege being here. When my friends knew that a visit to Crathie was to be on the agenda for this year, I wasn't short of advice. And the message that came over was that I shouldn't make the sermon political. "Just go with the lectionary readings" they said. And that is what I have done. I say this to make the point that it wasn't my idea to choose a passage that refers to planning a large public building without checking how much it was going to cost in the first place. And that's the last time I won't mention the Scottish parliament!

What a fascinating passage this is in Luke's gospel. It launches out in dramatic hyperbole, presenting what on the face of it is an impossible and scandalous challenge to anyone who wants to follow Jesus and be his disciple. Nothing but complete commitment is to be acceptable. Love of father or mother will get in the way of that and so must be jettisoned. Forget the commandment about honouring your father and mother. Even life itself is too much of a tempting distraction. Turn your back on it. All that is on offer is the way of the Cross: not an obvious way to get recruits for any cause other than dysfunctional masochists.

But then Jesus appeals to their real life experience. You wouldn't start out on an important undertaking, like building a tower or undertaking a military campaign, without calculating the cost carefully beforehand. Then neither should you slither into discipleship, sampling it for a bit and then giving it up when the going gets tough. And if you are serious about this undertaking, then the cost of it is no less than your whole life. And that's a measure of just how wonderful it is to be Jesus' disciple, to follow him and receive the life he offers.

There is something tantalisingly back to front about the logic here, something that doesn't fit. The world of faith and the world of public activity work in different ways, and so using the one to explain the other doesn't really work.

Luke anchors his argument in the commercial, political world. It is a calculating world, a world of reciprocal obligation, where you don't get something for nothing; a world of contracts between equals, a bilateral world; a pragmatic world where what matters is that things are made to happen. It's a world where everything can be planned and everything has its price.

But the world of faith is different. Earlier in the chapter from which today's reading comes, we have the stories of the great feast, where the host sends out invitations to his friends, gets ahead with planning a magnificent dinner, and then calls them to the table. Then the excuses start, the guest list evaporates and the host has to go out into the highways and byways to fill the places round the table.

Some years ago, a group used to meet to role play some of the gospel stories so as to explore their meaning more fully. They acted out that story, updating the excuses, and getting caught up in the drama. Till one of them put her finger on the problem. "It's not fair" she shouted. "If we could see the feast, we'd come!" But in the world of faith you can't see the feast. You have to take it on trust. In some ideal sense, the feast is what the people of faith are supposed to be modelling. Occasionally you get a glimpse of it in an exceptional life, but we know that even that will always be a pale imitation of what it is really like.

Each person who leads a faithful life has a chance to taste the feast. That is the same message as the promise of life in Deuteronomy. The choice in front of the people there is between doing God's will and not doing it, trusting that the way to a fulfilled life lies in that direction. It's like a recipe book without pictures. The end result has to be imagined. But at the same time, the disappointment is not so great when your misshapen offering doesn't match the professionally lit photograph you were hoping for. It probably tastes just as good!

Still, without the picture, how do you persuade people to set out as disciples? Luke's solution is to piggy-back on the contractual examples of building buildings and waging war. If the outcome is in proportion to the resources committed, then the joy of discipleship is so wonderful that it's worth your whole life. Indeed it's more wonderful than the life offered in Deuteronomy. It's of a different order than the faith of your mother and father; in such a different league that the old rules no longer apply.

But to leave it there is to miss half the story. To leave it there is to run the risk of treating the world of faith in contractual terms, to assume that we can measure the gift of the feast in terms of the size of the flowers or the weight of the chocolates we bring with us to as a gift for the host, to assume that there is an equivalence possible in the love God has for us and the love we can offer God.

And some people think that is the way it works. After the premiere of *The Passion of the Christ* folk were being interviewed on their way out of the cinema. One of them was quite overcome. "When I see how much he suffered and how much he loved me, I love him all the more" she said. I don't think it's like that. God is not giving us an invoice for the love he has for us. His love spills over in abundant, uncalculated generosity, requiring no pay back. And we keep forgetting that.

We need to read further. In the next chapter, Luke places the parables of God's unconditional love: the shepherd who behaves irresponsibly in our terms by leaving ninety nine of his sheep to go in search of the one he has lost, the father whose sons see his love as currency between them, an inheritance to be claimed, security to be hoarded, and both are bewildered then the father welcomes his wayward son back with open arms.

Alastair Moffat has written of the difference between his father and his mother. "She loved us first and asked questions later. He asked questions and then, if we supplied the right answer, then he might love us". God doesn't set us tests like Alastair Moffat's father, before loving us. And that is not a love we can reciprocate, though we can respond to it in committed service.

The worlds of faith and action may have different rules to them, but in the lives of committed disciples they come together in creative ways. And the horizon of the world of commerce and political reality are widened as its ethos of prudence and calculation is challenged. Debts are cancelled and the poor come into their proper inheritance. Justice is tempered with mercy, broken lives are healed, and false gods are dethroned. Miracles can happen and we forget that.

Walter Breuggemann releases us from the world of the calculated contract in his reflection on generosity:

> On our own we conclude;
> That there is not enough to go around
>
> We watch
> > And take food we did not grow and
> > Life we did not invent and
> > Future that is gift and gift and gift and

Families and neighbours who sustain us
When we don't deserve it.

By your giving, break our cycles of imagined scarcity
Override our presumed deficits
Quiet our anxieties of lack
Transform our perceptual field to see
The abundance, ...mercy upon mercy
Blessing upon blessing

Sink your generosity deep into our lives
That your muchness may expose our false lack
That endlessly receiving we may endlessly give
So that the world may be made Easter new.
Amen

Inscribing the Text: Sermons and Prayers
of Walter Brueggemann

Sunday September 5th 2004, Crathie Kirk

WORSHIP AND SERVICE

Luke 10:38-42; James 2:14-18;Psalm 150

Let everything that hath breath praise the Lord. Alleluia!

Most glorious Lord of Life
We relish the opportunity to praise you
We praise you
in metrical psalms
> in Gaelic lullabies
>
> in Peruvian Glorias
>
> in English Magnificats
>
> in Ukrainian Kyries
>
> in four-square harmony and lisping songs for children
>
> in all the crazy cacophony that love for you has
> inspired
>
> we praise your holy name.
> > Alleluia!

God of strength and of compassion
We sing your song of justice for those whom life has
discarded
> your song of comfort for those who mourn the loss of
> home or loved-ones
>
> your song of freedom for those suffocated by hatred
>
> your song of healing for the wounded
>
> your song of fulfilment for the poor and the hungry
>
> your song of dignity for those violated and
> stigmatised
and we sing in harmony with people of good will across
the world and down the years
in the great chorus that speaks of peace, your peace:

Let everything that hath breath praise the Lord.
Alleluia!

Loving Lord of Martha and of Mary
whose we are and whom we serve
we praise you in our service
    in our homes where old folk live with peace and
    dignity
    in our community projects; drop-in centres, Internet
    cafes, after-school clubs
    in learning from people with learning difficulties
    in welcoming refugees
    in walking alongside those walking away from
    dependency on drugs and
    alcohol
    in offering our resources to fight HIV/AIDS

Lord Jesus, we give you thanks for the privilege and the
opportunity and the resources to follow you in service.

Let everything that hath breath praise the Lord.
Alleluia!

Heavenly Father, at the start of our last day together, we
ask your blessing on our deliberations.
May we bring clear minds, open hearts and passionate
commitment to our task.
and grant us a speedy conclusion.

We ask it in Jesus' name. Amen.

*Friday May 21st when the General Assembly discussed worship and
social responsibility.*

FOR FESTIVALS

PALM SUNDAY

Palm Sunday is a day for the children. I used to feel a relief about getting to Palm Sunday after the introversion and anxiety of Lent. You knew where you were. *"Hosanna, loud Hosanna, the little children sang"*. Sunday School preparation was easy – palm leaves and stories about donkeys. *"We have a king who rides a donkey!"*

> Children of Jerusalem
> Sang the praise of Jesus' name
> Hark! Hark! Hark!
> While infant voices sing

The children tell you a lot about the crowd that day. Their presence tells you it was safe. There was a carnival atmosphere. "You can take the family". We use that as a measure of safety when we talk about football matches, or Orange parades. If children are there, nothing nasty is going to happen.

We're not very good in Scotland about combining religion and carnival, yet if you visit some of the great pilgrimage places in France, you can see that for centuries faith and commercial tourism have rubbed along happily together. And in Jerusalem in Jesus' day, Passover was a time when the city would have been bursting at the seams and partying.

Festivals and food often go together. Earlier this year, we were in Bangladesh at the time of a Muslim festival and we were stuck in an enormous traffic jam outside the cattle market, which was working overtime to provide meat for the festival. And for the Passover, you need a supply of lambs. The Roman author Josephus reckons that in one year, over a quarter of a million Passover lambs were slaughtered. If one lamb fed ten people, there must have been around three million pilgrims at the Passover festival.

So, where did they stay? They brought tents with them and camped in the fields and olive groves around the city. For the duration of the Passover, the area round the Mount of Olives was deemed to be part of Jerusalem itself, because pilgrims were expected to spend a minimum of one night in the city, and, since the city couldn't cope with them all, the boundaries had to be extended in order to accommodate them, in places like Bethphage and Bethany, over the shoulder of the Mount of Olives. Where the story begins.

When we think of all the crowds that were there, it's all the more surprising that Jesus' wee procession should have attracted so much attention. A couple of years ago, our church in Edinburgh joined forces for the morning service with the local Anglican and URC churches that we have a covenant with. We started in our own buildings and then processed in various directions along George IV Bridge, the Episcopal church carrying a large processional cross, which was used as an impromptu traffic lollipop to let us get across the road! At that time on a Sunday morning, there wasn't much traffic around, and there were a few encouraging smiles for us, but we hardly caused the commotion that we're told that Jesus and his disciples did.

That was because the Passover was supposed to be a "foot festival". It was supposed to involve effort. Some people walked for miles to get to

Jerusalem but even those who were camped outside the city had the chance to walk the last bit. So for Jesus, an apparently healthy young man, to ride into the city on an animal was unusual enough to attract comment. And to choose a donkey to do it was to signal to the Biblically literate in the crowd that this was no ordinary young man. They would know what Zechariah had said:

> Rejoice greatly, O daughter of Zion
> Shout aloud, O daughter of Jerusalem
> Lo, your king comes to you
> Triumphant and victorious
> Humble and riding on an ass

And that's where the political trouble of the week started. In raised expectations.

> All glory, laud and honour
> To thee, Redeemer, King

That hymn revels in the glory and the triumph of the day. In the hopes of the people rocketing sky-high. Their King had arrived. Salvation was at hand.

But not in the way they expected. The signals were there, even in that procession, the contradictions that later on in the week were going to blow the whole enterprise apart. That were going to generate a very different crowd. One where there were no children. One that would call for blood.

The hymn we've just sung anticipates that tension. Jesus' idea of leadership and kingship was not the same as theirs. The hymn talks of lowly pomp (a kind of Presbyterian idea). Of captive death. Of the powerful God bowing his meek head to mortal pain. It's honest about the paradoxes of the Christian story that anchors joy and hope and the celebration of God's transforming love in the reality of a world that, in too many ways, is separated from that love. A world of pain and exploitation, of squandered resources and misuse of power.

It's possible to present the Gospel as all comfort and self-regard. Some years ago, I visited some congregations that were "Bucking the trend" in that their membership was increasing. One of these was unusual in that in the service there were no prayers for the world, no prayers for anything other than the needs of that particular congregation.

These are what have been called "Palm Sunday Christians", Christians on the wrong side of the cross, with a cosy faith that finds it easy to give praise, a faith unchallenged by the world's pain. On the other side of the cross, next week on Easter Day, the praise has a different timbre to it. It is praise after scourging and death. It is praise of a God who suffered the worst his people could do to him, in order that he could give to all who suffer a future beyond suffering. The stories that follow Easter are ones that have to do with restoring and reconciling; with putting comfortable tradition and practice in its place and facing the world Easter new.

Between Palm Sunday and Easter Day, there was work to be done, self-interest to be challenged, the Kingdom to be anticipated in action. And the children were there too.

George MacLeod, the founder of the Iona Community, has a stunning meditation on the cleansing of the temple.

> In the temple, you threw out the money-changers, Lord Christ:

Down the steps and out of the door –
And into the vacant aisles came the children
Shouting for joy and dancing around.

George Macleod, The Whole Earth Shall Cry Glory

What a contrast! Between the careful, calculating officers of the institution, intent on sticking to the rules, rules that they had made, rules that favoured them and their interests. And on the other hand the exuberance of the children, letting the sunshine in, in their laughter and their noise.

The authorities didn't like it, particularly when they heard the children singing "Hosanna to the son of David". They gave Jesus a row but he reiterated the theme of so much of his teaching that God was more likely to be revealed to the weak and powerless than to those who thought they were at the centre of things.

Too often, we are the money-changers,
Giving short change in spiritual things
To many who seek the true coin:
Making the church an institute
When you want it to be a chaos of uncalculating love

George Macleod, The Whole Earth Shall Cry Glory

What a vision that is for the church! A chaos of uncalculating love. A place of generosity and welcome for all, noisy children, people in need of healing, the blind and the lame, where love and exuberance come first and God is worshipped fearlessly. A church that follows Christ out into the ever-changing world, to face new challenges and to be shaped by them.

Were these some of the dreams of those who set up the ecumenical parish forty years ago? Dreams of freedom to create something fresh, dreams of service and community, dreams of adventure and discovery? And was it dreams that kept them going through the difficult bits, or a strong belief that a new town called for a new church and that it would be wrong to short change the boldness of the town planners by offering them the tattered, battle-weary patchwork of a historically divided church?

I know it's not been an easy time but you have held to a vision that has also infected others. You are the flagship parish in Scotland and, in the autumn, at the special conference to be held here in the Lanthorn, you will have the chance to tell other ecumenical projects what it's been like. And to be thanked by them, for showing the way and for staying the course. And to join with them in the challenge of renewing the church we love.

> Drive out from our hearts
> Our calculated offerings
> Our easy responses
> And let child-like faith
> Flood into us again

> George Macleod, The Whole Earth Shall Cry Glory

Sunday March 20th 2005, St Columba's Livingston.

REMEMBRANCE

We gather today to pay tribute to those who have lost their lives in warfare. We are surrounded by a memorial built by those who believed they had fought the war to end all wars, yet we are in mourning for the dead of today's war in Iraq. Uppermost in our minds is bound to be the Black Watch, facing an uncertain future as a regiment: a regiment with a distinguished history, putting their soldiers' skill and courage on the line in a war born out of violence and oppression that has claimed thousands of lives. Our prayers are with them and with their families in this time of fear and of uncertainty. And we pray also for the people of Iraq, hurtling from tragedy to tragedy as they long for peace in their beautiful land.

Today is a very precious day. I didn't used to think so. Remembrance Day used to be a day when I got angry. Angry at any hint that God was only on our side. Angry at the repetition of imagery and thought forms from the First World War that seemed to have little to say to someone born after the Second. Angry that there seemed to be no place for the dilemmas of my generation. Angry, I think, because I didn't understand how I fitted into this picture, a picture of alien passions that embarrassed me.

Today, I believe that Remembrance Day is precious. Through the stories of particular people and the memories of those whose lives have been turned upside down by war, we have a chance to try to understand where we all fit into the dark picture of these passions and fears that refuse to be tamed and that still haunt our TV screens and our consciences.

The grief we feel at the deaths of Scottish soldiers in Iraq opens up the whole warren of warfare. It links the experience of people like myself, brought up during the Cold War, protected from personal contact with the gashes that war tears in a life, with those for whom the horrific memory of war lives quietly and persistently with them all their days. Those whose lives and loves have been wrecked by war. Those whose decisions can wound or heal, can mean life or death for someone. Those who have committed their lives to serve in the armed forces and live with the possibility of being killed in battle. Those whose names are on this or other memorials.

Remembrance Day is a day when each person faces their own kind of vulnerability in the face of the raw violence of the human ingredients of inhuman warfare, relationships gone wrong, rights ignored, ambition flexing its muscles.

That gap between people's experience of war is notoriously difficult to bridge. War reporters and cameramen spread the illusion that we know what's going on. But despite our sophisticated means of communication, we just don't get it.

Yet we must try. We are the beneficiaries of that democracy for which today's war is being fought in Iraq and for which young lads from Fife and from other parts of the world are being killed and that imposes responsibilities on us. It is being fought in our name and we must try to understand its passions so that we can keep asking the questions "Why are they there? What is it for? What will come of it?"

Our reading comes from a series of five chapters in St John's Gospel which have the recurring theme of Jesus trying to make his disciples understand what he is going through as he sees the end of his earthly life approaching. His words are dominated by thoughts of love, the love between himself and God, his love for his disciples, their love for each other. By what he can still do for them, through the Holy Spirit. By the selflessness of love, by its refusal to be limited, even by death. You can hear the desperation of his need to communicate as he repeats himself, paraphrases his main points, tries to shock them, then to comfort them. Yet he fails to get through. His disciples are unable to enter his world where every action, every thought has an immediacy and a significance because time is running out for him.

When I visited Sandhurst earlier this month, I was given a lovely book of pictures and reflections. Here's one of them:

> Life is not a dress rehearsal.
> We should seize the day; we shouldn't waste time.
> We should try to find the mystery of our lives and not
> leave it too late.

Each day is a precious gift, and it places on all of us the responsibility to use it well, with clear purpose. Life isn't a dress rehearsal, the drama is now. And it's not a repeat, either. In an asymmetric war, where unassailable American might faces the incomprehensible recklessness of the suicide bomber, we can't rely on the formulae of the past. We must dig deep into the resources of our faith and refashion them for today's need.

Where do we start? On the morning after the attacks on the Twin Towers, Rowan Williams reflected on how we should respond to the language of hatred and violence that had been articulated that day. If we choose to continue the conversation in the same language of violence and hatred, we will be drawn deeper and deeper into the hatreds of those who hate us. And we will become imprisoned by them. Perhaps that's what Jesus meant when he said we should love our enemies. It's only the language of love and peace that releases any of us from a spiral of death and injustice.

What might that mean? Well, when this awful war is over, I hope that the image that we remember is that of the British soldiers patrolling without their helmets in Basra. It's a powerful, and a complex image. It expresses a commitment to building peace, and breaking the cycle of conflict. It encapsulates the vulnerability that is part of building trust. It shows the professionalism that can take risks. Perhaps it even transforms the skills of war into the tools of peace.

Jesus said, "This is my commandment, that you love one another as I have loved you." That kind of love isn't comfortable and doesn't have quick results. But nothing else can heal our torn world.

November 11th 2004, National War Memorial, Edinburgh Castle.

CHRISTMAS DAY

Yea, Lord, we greet Thee
Born this happy morning;
Jesus, to Thee be glory given

Martin Luther said "Christians are blissful people who can rejoice at heart and sing praises, stamp and dance and leap for joy". And at Christmas, we sing and rejoice more than ever. It was the angels that started it, praising God and saying, "Glory to God in the highest, and on earth peace toward men" a great hymn of praise to God, expressing for all of us the wonderful liberating surge of joy that we feel when faced with God's glory. And they heralded the birth of the Prince of Peace, of that peace that only God can give and that speaks to the heart of each one of us.

Over the centuries the subtleties and the hidden corners of the Christmas story have been celebrated in song, and carol and great set piece choral work. They've been belted out by brass bands, piped out over supermarket tannoy systems, whispered by nursery children in nativity plays, shouted by carol singers over the competing noise in shopping malls. There's not a dry eye in the house as a wee tot sings a solo of "Away in a manger". Carols keep up the spirits of the band collecting for the homeless or AIDS orphans. Shopping tills trill along all the more enthusiastically to the sound of "Do they know it's Christmas?" Music and singing are an integral part of Christmas.

As they are of our faith. Hugh MacDiarmid referred to the realm of music as "the gate which separates the earthly from the eternal". And at Christmas we can hear that gate swung boldly open as the choir reveals mysteries in the Christmas story that words simply mask, or as the tears flow yet again when we sing a particular line of a well loved carol. There's some kind of communication with the eternal that only music can mediate.

One voice of that communication is praise. The Bible is full of praise. Praise to God, Creator of heaven and earth, provider of all good things, redeemer of his people. It's a large part of the psalms. These days, our praise of the Creator is heightened by an appreciation of the intricate ecological balancing of need and provision, coloured by the drama of apathy, desperation and self-interest that mediates our relationship with the created world. We recognise the fugue that develops between the first voice of the world entrusted to us by God; the dramatic entry of the mystery of Christ's birth, death and resurrection that sheds new light on that relationship; and the later themes formed by our own technological creativity.

And throughout, we are accompanied by the voice of the artist, the poet, the musician, as they name the damage done, spark in us an appreciation of the glory that's at risk, and lead us through the motivational quagmire of human relationships in a magnificent but fragile world. They help us to see with our ears and listen with our eyes, as God's glory is revealed to us.

But praise is only one mode of our dialogue with God. The psalms are also full of complaint, despair, arrogance, contentment, the currency of the personal emotions that are engendered by belief in and dependency on a distant God. Within the Christmas story itself, we have a couple of these personal psalms, the *Magnificat* and *Nunc Dimittis*, beloved of Anglican evensong, the songs of Mary and of Simeon.

Simeon sang for joy, shortly after Jesus' birth. He was an old man who had waited all his life to see the Messiah, and there he was, a baby in his arms. His was a quiet, personal joy, thankful that he had lived to see this moment. It was the joy of recognition, of understanding that a light had come into the world that the darkness would never snuff out.

And there was Mary. The angel had just told her that she was going to be the Mother of God's son. Nobody else knew this and it was truly momentous news. People had been longing for the Messiah for ages, so she had been let into a real secret. But what was even more amazing was the way this wonderful event was going to happen. Not in a palace, or to the great and the good, but to a simple girl. And that meant that big changes were on the way. The world was never going to be the same again. No wonder she couldn't keep from singing.

So part of the musical repertoire at Christmas is praise of and response to God. But part of it is also a dialogue between ourselves, as we try to fathom the mystery of Christmas.

On Wednesday evening, I was at a Service of Nine Lessons and Carols in St Mary's Cathedral. One of the pieces the choir sang was *God Is With Us,* by John Tavener, which I hadn't heard before. The text was familiar, largely Isaiah 9, but the music was awesome. A friend said afterwards that through it you looked down into a great cavern of undiscovered meaning in the words of a story you thought you knew. The reason the Christmas story endures is because of these layers of meaning that the words pretend to reveal but don't. And over the centuries music has sometimes opened them up for us in fresh ways.

We shouldn't be surprised by this. Christmas is all about new ways of communicating, about the Word being made flesh, about God walking through the gate between the earthly and the eternal and taking human form, the better to share the good news of God's love for the world.

God is with us, no longer a distant deity.

And that was just the start, the start of new kinds of encounter with God. Encounters that continue today, as we meet Christ in the bread and wine of communion.

> Word of the Father,
> Now in flesh appearing,
> O come let us adore him, Christ the Lord.

December 25th 2004, Greyfriars and Highland Tolbooth Kirk, Edinburgh.

IN THE WAKE OF THE TSUNAMI

SEEING FOR MYSELF

How do you make human links between people in Scotland and those
whose lives have been devastated by the tragedy of the tsunami? Just
after Christmas, our family went to *Kiss me Kate* in the Edinburgh
Festival Theatre and the audience were filling buckets with donations
for the victims before the performance and again at the end. That
memory of open sympathy stayed with me on this visit as we met
fishermen on the east coast of India and in Sri Lanka who lost
everything when the big wave hit. Everywhere we went, I tried to
convey to people how deeply folk in Scotland were affected, their wish
to help and to know more about the tragedy.

We'd seen the devastation already on the television. But it's quite
different looking out over the wide, flat horizon of the sea while the
man beside you is reliving the time when he looked out and saw it
turned into a wall of water. Or seeing the two parts of a brightly
decorated fishing boat lying fifty yards from each other, as if it had
been sawn in half. You walk across the beach and see stuffed holdalls
or part of a broken electrical appliance or clothes or lids of jars sticking
through the sand.

In one of the villages, staff from a local advertising agency were
helping with the clean-up operation and a tiny boy was doing his bit,

carrying small pieces of broken concrete across to a pile of debris, supervised by his slightly bigger brother. They came from a beach slum, on the wrong side of the railway track.

We met people who had had miraculous escapes. Some families had been separated when the wave came. A mother, who was light enough, managed to cling to a ceiling fan, while her husband was carried out of the room, clutching their two year old son. A young boy played *Coulter's Candy* for us on his violin and then a piece he'd composed for his teacher, who'd been lost. An older woman spoke of how a young cousin, who had lost her husband and two children, was wandering along the coast, visiting every hospital, in search of the son whose body had not been found.

Locally, the response was immediate. Networks were mobilised and the roads filled with vehicles loaded with supplies. Sri Lanka was already well provided with relief and emergency organisations, still working in the country because of the twenty year civil war. UNHCR, UNICEF, the Red Cross, and other large international NGOs quickly switched from development to relief mode and the Government set about co-ordinating the whole operation. Aid and money have been pouring in since the tragedy. We heard that as many as 300 organisations without a direct base in the country have arrived to help.

It's difficult to separate fact from rumour but it seems that the rescue and relief efforts have been remarkably successful. The damage has been mapped, although the number missing keeps changing, as does the number dead. People who were sheltering in schools are being moved out so that the schools can reopen on Monday. The threat of cholera and other diseases has so far been averted. The focus now is on the medium and long term provision.

It's still a mystery why people have responded so generously in this case. Somehow this has penetrated our self-absorption so that we want to try to identify with complete strangers in their grief.

Perhaps the basic ingredients of the tragedy are so fundamental that they sweep aside the differences in circumstances between people. The effects were completely arbitrary, showing no favours. The fishermen we spoke to commented that cyclones are just as devastating and they are used to them, but they can see them coming and so take avoiding action. But this struck without warning. For some, it seemed to tear up various rule books that gave shape to their lives, shattering trust and security as it went. People told us that in these parts they think of the sea as their mother and they were bewildered to see her turn into such a destructive force. It exposed the essential vulnerability that all people have in common.

The logistical distance between the people who can give in Scotland and the people in need is far greater than the emotional one. On the whole, the people most affected are those who are and always have been at the end of the line, whether the line is bureaucratic, or economic, or humanitarian. The strong instinct to give in kind, sending things we think the people there will need, shows that people want to minimise the length of that line between donor and recipient.

It's not so easy, however. The large agencies are set up to cope efficiently with the emergency needs. We saw large chests being delivered to the UNICEF office. Each contained a kit of basic educational supplies for eighty children and they had enough to ensure that the schools would have what they needed to open next week. Once the emergency is over, pencils and jotters and chalk can be provided locally.

On the whole, although it does need money, a country like Sri Lanka already has the material and human resources to cope, and using them is preferable to bypassing the local economy. Immediately after the disaster, the Scots Kirk in Colombo was asked to find sheets for a small community that they work with on the coast. They bought a bolt of cloth and gave it to women in a local sewing project to hem, allowing them to get the benefit of the sale as well as an opportunity to make their own contribution to the relief effort.

Providing houses and schools and sanitation is relatively straightforward but there's also a huge job to be done in healing wounded people and communities. It's likely that some 60% of the people who have died were children so the problems are not so much orphaned children as bereaved parents and this is an area where outside help is welcome, in order to train local counsellors. Lots of fishermen say they are afraid to go back to sea, so it may not be a question of simply restoring what was there before. We heard that students at the Theological College of Lanka are devising street theatre to help communities come to terms with what has happened.

Everyone we met was keen to get it right, to ensure that the response was driven by people's real needs and hopes rather than a grand blueprint, but also that it was well co-ordinated so that communities didn't get missed out and that organisations didn't duplicate their efforts. That won't happen overnight, so a bit of patience is called for at present until we see who's taking responsibility for what. In the meantime, the political agenda during Britain's presidency of the G8 will give ample opportunity to promote a more sustainable future for many of the affected countries. I hope in the longer term we can build on the goodwill that the disaster has generated and keep a close interest in the lives and prospects of people in these areas.

Published in The Scotsman on 14th January 2005.

WHERE GOD FITS INTO THE STORIES

When I left for India and Sri Lanka, I packed a couple of books of theological reflections on September 11th. The tsunami was of course a natural disaster, not immediately the outcome of human intention, but it seemed to be a world changing event of the same order as 9 11. And many of the challenges that it posed to people of faith were similar.

- Where was God in the tragedy and its aftermath?

That question tests our faith, no matter how we understand God or the spiritual realm.

- On both occasions our essential vulnerability was exposed in the face of overwhelming power.

This raised the question of what resources our faith could offer in these circumstances.

- In both cases, we had to face up to the global injustices and inequalities that the events revealed – it was the fishing villages, not the beach resorts that were generally washed away.

- Both events were unpredicted and that came as a shock to us all. It showed how fundamental our assumptions are that there is an order to the world and that we have a handle on it, and often that handle is given by faith as much as by science.

After September 11th, people asked whether things would ever be the same again. Similarly, we can ask what has changed since December 26th. Have we learnt anything from the experience? Or is it just business as usual?

Let's start with the fishermen we met on the east coast of India, in Tamil Nadu. We were told that twenty villages down the coast had been devastated by the wave and we saw some of the wrecks of the houses. Many of them had been made simply of walls of mud and matting, with a thatched roof of woven coconut palm leaves and the only evidence that anyone had lived there were scattered possessions poking through the sand. Other houses were concrete, and in many cases all that remained were the foundations, with stray slabs of bits of walls littering the beach.

The broken boats told a more significant story, stranded in fields or caught in among the palm trees. And beside them, ruined nets. Nets are very expensive. One net might weigh 500 kilos and we were told that one kilo of netting costs around 300 rupees (£3.50). They have different kinds of nets for different kinds of fish. It wasn't just the material shells of lives that had gone: people's livelihoods had been washed away. Replacing nets and boats would be hugely expensive and there was a concern that compensation would go to the owners rather than the fishermen themselves.

The zeal of politicians to prevent such a tragedy again isn't always a help and it's in danger of producing a quagmire of regulation. In Sri Lanka, the Government was proposing to enforce a regulation that prevents building houses within 300 metres of the sea and, instead, designing flatted housing inland. There was huge scepticism about whether this would work and concern about how fishing villages would survive. And I'm sure many families in this city would echo these anxieties about whether it's advisable to uproot communities in this way, supposedly for their own good.

But it wasn't only the cost and the management of change that was an issue. The community had lost its nerve. We were told in India that, right along the coast, people thought of the sea as their mother and that mother had turned to murdering her children. That was hard to take. Fishermen said they didn't want to go back to the sea. One afternoon in Colombo, we noticed a small group standing on the beach, staring together out to sea, as if trying to reconnect with it. These communities won't be re-established in a hurry. And in the meantime, the communities themselves will change as new working patterns and new social structures emerge to replace the ones lost in the wave.

The shape of the communities has changed, because the wave culled at random, but, as always, it tended to take the weak before the strong. One priest said he'd buried three hundred children. In cultures where single parenthood is frowned upon, there's a lot of readjusting to do and, as new families are formed, there's a fear that some of the remaining children will slip through the net and be abandoned. In the end of the day, these communities will catch up with themselves and resume their role in fishing and tourism, but it won't be for some time. The tsunami has cut a great gash in their history and there's a lot of healing to be done.

We met some people who'd had miraculous escapes. It was the holiday season so lots of people had left Colombo for the coast and were settling down for a rest by the sea.

One couple with a two year old son were separated, the boy with his father clinging on to him as he grasped at trees to escape from the wave, the mother hanging on to a ceiling fan as the water rose up in the room, with nowhere else to go.

A teenage girl had gone off in search of some riding equipment and her family searched for two hours before being reunited with her.

Another couple were more anxious about the fate of their daughter who had gone sailing in the Maldives than with the drama of their own rescue by a local family deep in the jungle.

Some were still in deep shock, unable to talk about it. Others couldn't stop talking, trying to cope with pain and incredulity and anger, fixing their experience and their reaction in words that they wouldn't forget.

One father ran a business hiring out windsurfing equipment and developing other kinds of water sports. His shock was the bewilderment of a professional who thought he understood the sea. How could this happen? Why had it not been predicted? His life depended on the sea being manageable. He wrestled with it, played with it, and there was a sense of betrayal in his reaction, as if the sea had not played by the rules.

The mother whose daughter was away sailing prayed incessantly until she heard she was safe, and also berated herself for the silly rows they'd had over trivial things. The tsunami set new standards of care, provided a different yardstick against which to measure what is important in life.

These stories are important because, in some sense, we are all survivors of this tragedy. I'm sure we've all felt a sense of gratitude that we are safe, a sense of our own smallness and fragility in the face of the might of natural forces, a need to reach out and connect with those immediately affected.

And that brings me to what has been called the second wave, the wave of compassion and generosity, expressed in donations to development and aid charities. A world weary with the endless, relentless growth of global poverty seemed to see here a tangible need, something that could be done. And the money rolled in.

We met several people tasked with receiving and spending this money. Many of the faith communities were quick off the mark, going straight to places they knew that were in need. Sadly, they have plenty of experience in dealing with disasters in that part of the world. In India, the delivery mechanisms from the Gujerat earthquake were quickly put in place again. Sri Lanka was already well supplied with the large agencies, UN, ICRC, and several large development charities, who were there because of the recent civil war and its aftermath. They already had people who knew the culture and the language and they quickly moved gear from reconstruction and capacity building to relief and rescue.

An urgent need was to sort out the ecology of the aid effort. When we visited the UNICEF offices, they had just taken delivery of crates of school supplies. Each crate had enough classroom equipment for 80 children. This would see them through the first term, until normal service resumed, and they had enough for the whole island. Impressive and necessary at that juncture, because it was important to get the schools opened as soon as possible.

But it also demonstrated the weakness of the large agencies. They are all top down in their approach, not immediately geared to addressing the individual needs of communities and people. Smaller charities and faith communities are better connected on the ground, so each needs the other and co-ordinating the response is important. That will take time, so as donors we have to be patient.

Yet this was one of the anxieties added to the shoulders of aid workers, many of whom were at worrying levels of exhaustion when we met them. They worried that disillusion would set in if their donors didn't see results quickly. And that would be bad news the next time an emergency happened. Locally, people were concerned that their own economy would suffer if the market was flooded with goods they were used to supplying. There was a battle going on, or a battle anticipated, over what was going to be in the driving seat - the needs of the donors, or the needs of the recipients.

And that poses a very fundamental challenge to our understanding of generosity and solidarity. Where does trust lie in either of these? I suspect we're not good at seeing the difference between a generosity that releases the gift into the hands of the other, and a transaction where we retain control of our resources. It's complicated, of course, by corruption, and we have to be careful not to line the pockets of those who will exploit the situation. Giving a donation wisely and generously is a complicated business.

But the response has been so enormous that it also speaks to a need on our part. There's also something wrong with a response that pays up and leaves it at that. We have to find some way of preserving that connectedness between people across the continents and allowing it to live.

On the face of it, it's about death. Death of people, death of communities, death of security and innocence. I came across this the other day:

> "Death, human death, is an outrage ... Most people will
> agree that there is something shocking in the death of a
> child, who has not had a chance even to live out her whole

human life-cycle; but I think that, in one way, every death cuts off a story that has infinite possibilities ahead of it"

Herbert McCabe, Catholic theologian

We can grieve for what might have been and we do. But can we plan for what could still be? Faith doesn't allow death to have the final say. There are still infinite possibilities for building something new, for healing the grief, for learning from the tragedy. We have heard what spiritual resources the faith communities have to set alongside the material resources already pledged. Let us work together to use them wisely.

January 23rd 2005, Inter-Faith Gathering at the University of Glasgow.

A TEST OF LOVE AND TRUST
Exodus 17: 1-7; Psalm 95; John 4: 4-15

"God is not a municipal authority."
So said the *Times of India* last month in a report which outlined some of the theological comment that was around on the devastating tsunami. Faced with indiscriminate destruction on that scale, religion was on trial. How could a good God, a just God allow such a thing? Who is this God you expect us to believe in?

In the context of the unspeakable desolation of that tragedy, these questions were probably a symptom of despair, rather than its cause, even if the feeling of being abandoned by God no doubt aggravated how lost people felt. On top of losing their livelihood and their family, fishermen in India were stunned that the sea that they had regarded as their mother should turn against them in this way. This wave that was of Biblical proportions sent us all back to our Bibles, to read them in a new light and to think again about the God in whom we believed.

In many cases, the commentator's outlook was unaffected, the tragedy simply amplifying the characteristics of the God that they had previously believed in, be it a vengeful God, or a sorrowing God, or an inscrutable God. In the case of some observers, faith was shattered. In all cases, it was challenged. And in the countless lives torn apart by the wave, robbed of confidence, hope, security, the very means of survival, the journey to spiritual restoration has only begun.

Ancient questions wrenched out of people's anger and despair. Questions that were being asked in the wilderness by God's chosen people, God's pampered people, God's insecure people. In their case, it was *lack* of water that was the problem. After escaping from

Pharaoh's army, which we are told had been engulfed by a huge wave, things had not been going smoothly. At Marah, they had found water that they couldn't drink until Moses threw a stick into it, as ordered by God, and that removed its bitter taste. They had needed to be fed with quails and manna in the desert and here they were, thirsty again. Again, they bullied God through Moses till water came from the rock and they could drink.

This is a story that carries both emotional and intellectual messages. At its heart, it's all a test. A test of love and a struggle for survival. The Hebrew people had seen what God had done to the Egyptians. If they'd picked up the wrong message in believing that they were God's special people, then they were playing with fire. They needed to be reassured of God's special love, and so they set up hoops for God to jump through. No matter how often the trick was done, they asked for more. The way they looked at it, unless God gave them what they asked for, they concluded that God did not love them and then they were in trouble.

It's a tussle for trust. And it shows that trust isn't something that can be gained simply by action. Being trusted is different from being seen to be reliable. In those days in the wilderness, they knew that God had stood by them time and time again and yet they still needed reassurance.

Psalm 95, which is also part of today's lectionary readings, picks up this same story of God being tested in the desert and sets it in the context of God's creative power and faithful care. God is faithful to the caring and loving relationship with Creation, although it may not be possible to predict how that will be demonstrated. We often sing the first part, a magnificent psalm of praise for our Creator God who protects the people of his pasture.

O come, let us sing to the Lord;

Let us make a joyful noise to the rock of our salvation!

For the Lord is a great God,

And a great king above all gods.

In his hands are the depths of the earth;

The heights of the mountains are his also.

The sea is his for he made it,

And the dry land which his hands have formed.

But there's a sting in the tail that portrays how peeved God had been over this incident at Meribah.

Do not harden your hearts, as at Meribah,

When your ancestors tested me

And put me to the proof, though they had seen my work.

For forty years, I loathed that generation.

That's because God is not a municipal authority, at the beck and call of everyone, ready to dance to the tunes that we play. Perhaps it's only at times of crisis that we revert to the expectation that God should be like this. Most of the time, we believe in the "*Ordinary God*" as Donald Davie's poem puts it.

… events

He does not, it seems, determine

For the most part. Whether He could

Is not to the point; it is not

Stupid to believe in

A God who mostly abjures.

The ordinary kind

Of God is what one believes in

So implicitly that
It is only with blushes or
Bravado that one can declare
"I believe"; caught as one is
In the ambush of personal history, so
Harried, so distraught.

The ordinary kind
Of undeceived believer
Expects no prompt reward
From an ultimately faithful
But meanwhile preoccupied landlord.

Donald Davie, To Scorch or Freeze

The God who appears to rampage through human history, intervening on behalf of some and not others, turns out to be a strange father, a father who did not use that power on behalf of his own son. The God we find in the pages of the New Testament, and indeed in many of the Old, is the God who abjures and who weeps with those who suffer. Who feeds them, not with the comfort they crave, but with living water so that they never thirst again.

The story at Meribah has an intellectual dimension to it as well. It's not just the lack of trust that's insulting to God, it's the idea that we specify precisely how God should care for us, that we should reduce God to our own level of responsiveness. And that impulse runs deep in all of us.

It's a rare thing to find the trust that completely hands over control of events because that goes against our human instinct. Just in order to keep the wheels of normal interaction between people oiled, we often need to build up a picture of the kind of person we are dealing with, a picture that allows us to predict how they're going to behave and what things they care about. We tend to build up theories about other people and relate to these, rather than allowing them to be themselves and change and be inconsistent and surprise us.

One of the difficult periods in my life was when my mother was very ill. My brother lived far away and I had to give him regular reports of how she was and how she was coping. I had to explain her, box her into my understanding of what she was going through, which was something so dreadful I couldn't possibly share it with her. That need to articulate our relationship so that it could be communicated to somebody else, to reduce precious moments of closeness and of irritation to words was inimical to allowing the love and trust to flow freely that were so important at that time.

"They put God to the test." Rather than allowing God to stretch their understanding, they checked out whether God would measure up to the limited expectations they had of God's power. And in so doing they risked missing clues to the greater gifts God had in store for them.

One of the hardest lessons to accept, whether as believers, or scientists, or simply human beings getting to know each other, is that it's when the theory doesn't match the data that our understanding grows. It's when people surprise us, by going against what we expect, that we get to know them better. And it's when God puzzles us that we come closer to God, whether it's when we're hungry and thirsty in the desert, or turned inside out by a devastating natural disaster.

This university has been a place where understanding has grown over the centuries and today we celebrate those founders and benefactors who have made this proud tradition possible. It's a place where people have cultivated the ability to listen and look attentively, so that the reading that stubbornly sticks out of the pattern, or the response that goes against the trend can provide the clue to their next discovery. The most creative researchers are surely those who believe that the object of their study will always be one step ahead of them, leading them on to an ever deeper understanding.

So too in the Bible, God is always ahead of us, beyond our reach but beckoning us on. Beckoning us on into a richer, more intricate relationship of love and trust than our limited imaginations could ever map out. That's the living water that goes on refreshing us so that we may never thirst again.

February 27th 2005, Commemoration of Benefactors in St Salvator's Chapel, The University of St Andrew.

TALKS

POWER, PASSION AND POSSIBILITY

The Church in the Twenty-First Century

I often find myself saying this year that this is an exciting time for the church. In Western Europe, we enter this century apparently weaker in numbers and clout than we were in the last one, yet there is a great liberation in that. One of the most exciting books I have read recently is called "*The Death of Christian Britain*" by the Glasgow historian Callum Brown. Not an auspicious title. But what he was documenting was the demise of a particular culture that had held sway for too long unchallenged. A culture that was judgmental, because it had a superstitious hold over people; puritanical, in that it cared about outward appearances of respectability without questioning what was hiding behind that respectability; and discriminatory in its treatment of women. It's a culture that, nonetheless, had gems and pearls within it; it's the culture that nurtured me, and doubtless many of us here. Yet it served to disguise what I believe to be the essence of the Gospel and I do not mourn its passing, or at least its attenuation.

The church enters this century less encumbered by expectations about its social power. I recall the presentation by a Scandinavian youth delegate at the First European Ecumenical Assembly in Basel, in 1989. Her theme was "Take up your bed and walk" and she commented that this was much easier if you had a sleeping bag than if your bed was a water bed!

Part of the church's current context is anxiety about religion in general At an ecumenical brainstorming session in Lambeth recently, one church leader summed up the situation by saying that "For most people in public life, their default position is that religion is bad for you." And after the horrors of 9 11, the record of religious wars, and the petty wrangling among churches, I have to say that often they have a point.

But we believe that we do have something to offer the world around us, and not just the consolations of personal faith, but an enrichment of public life. And it matters how we make this contribution.

Acting together

More and more the pressure on churches to act and speak together is strong. Scotland is still haunted by the sectarianism of its past and, to a lesser extent, of its present. Last month, the Scottish Executive held a Summit on Sectarianism, inviting representatives from the churches, the football teams, the education authorities and the press to share their perspectives. It was a good meeting and something that could not have been envisaged ten, or even five years ago.

The ecumenical climate in Scotland is good. I have made a point this year, while I'm Moderator, of continuing to chair the Scottish Churches Forum, the governing body of the Scottish ecumenical instrument. It's fairly well accepted that sectarianism is less an issue of poor relationships between the churches than the sport of fringe groups. Yet there is still the danger of accentuating the divisions between communities in the way that we present differences of view. In what I hope was an illustration of good practice, the Catholic Church and the

Church of Scotland that week had issued a joint press release on the proposals for Family Law, acknowledging the differences between us, but setting them in the context of all that we agreed about and were doing together.

Communicating the Gospel

The temptation to resort to the power games of recent years is strong. Remember the Peanuts cartoon where Lucy shouts "Do you understand?" Charlie Brown puts his hands over his ears. "Yes, I understand! You don't have to yell at me!" Lucy reflects "Perhaps you're right….perhaps I shouldn't yell at you so much, but I feel that if I talked to you quietly as I am doing now…" (and again she shouts) *"you'd never listen"*.

We in the church are disciples of one of the greatest teachers of all time, whose power to communicate brought people out in their droves to listen to him. And he taught in parables, stories that "told it slant" that invited his listeners in to share the truths that they contained, that made them partners in the discovery of the pearls of the Gospel. Yet we distrust that tradition, as Christopher Driver said forty years ago:

> "The church, of course, has always deeply distrusted Jesus' reprehensible affection for parables. Its instinct (read any papal encyclical, listen to any Billy Graham campaign) has always been to lay 'truth' on the line and turn up the volume… But as any serious artist knows, the truth then ceases to be the truth. By being too accessible, it pierces no resistance, evokes no discernment".

We often think that, in order to enhance our intellectual and political credibility, we should eschew the picture, or the story, failing to recognise the similarities between the intellectual and the spiritual journey. There is more imaginative richness in other ways of knowing than we usually give them credit for. Pictures and stories help to explain things, whether you call them parables, or diagrams, or theories. So we should keep our nerve and take our lead from Jesus of Nazareth and not from the socio-political world in which we are embedded.

But the urge to conform to a managerial, supposedly scientific way of doing things goes further than our conceptual mind-set. Speaking twenty five years ago, at his enthronement as Archbishop of Canterbury, Robert Runcie said:

> "The temptation to gain the Church's end by using the world's means is still with us. We are tempted to organise ourselves like any other party or pressure group, to establish sharper dividing lines between those who are members and those who are not, to compete more aggressively for attention from the public, to recruit new members with a strident self –confidence which suggests we have nothing to learn, to persuade with a loud voice rather than with the quiet reason of the heart...
>
> We have spiritual treasure in the words of life; but it matters desperately how our treasure is shared, how those ends are pursued and how the Church seeks to exercise authority."

                              Robert Runcie, Windows into God

It matters how the treasure is shared. For starters, there is nothing intrinsically wrong with listening to those in society who are charged with packaging, marketing, selling various goods. To ignore their wisdom would be perverse. But the danger is that, in following their lead, we lose sight of what we are communicating.

Selling the Church

Another picture, this time from T S Eliot. There's a sign outside a Bakers' Shop advertising bread for $1 a loaf. So you go into the shop, hungry for bread and imagining the fresh smell of it, newly baked, only to discover that inside the shop all that is for sale are copies of the sign advertising bread for $1 a loaf. And Eliot suggests that the church is like that shop.

The danger is when we become apologists for the church instead of communicators of the Gospel. And when our measure of being faithful is how many people we can bring in through the church door. There is the danger there that we distort the nature of the church to make it attractive and comfortable, rather than trusting in the inherent attractiveness of the Gospel itself.

Some years ago, I presented a series of radio programmes called "Bucking the Trend" about churches in Scotland which were actually growing, in the narrow sense of increasing their membership. One church we visited had been facing imminent closure fifteen years before. When I asked the minister how he had turned the church's fortunes round, he told me that he had asked everyone attending the church under the age of forty to ask a number of their friends what sort of church they would come to. They reported what their friends had said. The minister said "We asked people what sort of church they wanted, and then made sure we gave it to them".

This is an illustration of church, religion and faith, as consumption. Grace Davie, the English sociologist of religion has remarked on this trend, a trend away from religion as obligation. Religion as obligation has dominated church-going in many parts of Europe (and I imagine of North America) for centuries. And, although we must not lose sight of the demands that faith puts on people, I expect that few would wish to return to an age when people went through the motions of religious commitment simply out of a sense of obligation. But is churchgoing as consumption much of an improvement?

Another community I visited for these radio programmes met in a school hall, and was part of the "cell church" movement. What staggered me was the fact that there was not a single prayer offered for anyone suffering in the world, and this, as it happens, in the week when the television news had been dominated by floods in Mozambique. When I asked the minister why there were no prayers for others, he said "That's not where we are on our spiritual journey". What was not clear was what was going to progress their spiritual journey away from their own needs.

The Edinburgh University teacher Ruth Page has pointed out that basing the church (mainly) where we *live* rather than where we *work* perhaps lies at the root of the disparity between two views of the church and its mission. Because the church traditionally operates where people live, what people bring to the church tends to be the concerns of their private lives, their families, the communities to which they belong. Perhaps one of the dilemmas for the church is the change in what communities people identify with. But, were the church much more to be found where people *work*, it might well be the much more public, social, political dimensions of living which were allowed to be addressed by the Gospel.

On the face of it, this movement of the church out from the concerns of a congregation to the needs of the world outside it, lies at the heart of the idea of the "Church without Walls". This is the short-hand name for a report to our General Assembly four years ago, which was taking stock of the role and mission of the Church of Scotland. It recommended that the church should become more local and relational in its outlook and the idea has caught on well. I suspect that a large part of its success lies in the different interpretations people can put on it. Many of us read it as an encouragement to a kind of ministry that's more on other people's territory, while others tend to see it as encouraging a kind of raiding party that launches out to drag more people back inside these very walls again.

This resistance to an outward looking faith, centred on other people's needs, came through in a survey undertaken recently for the Religious Broadcasting Department of BBC Scotland.

The research was conducted among people aged 35-45, all of whom had said they were interested in spiritual issues. In the first place, the research showed a distinct aversion to anything which smacked of institutional religion. That in itself isn't necessarily surprising. I recognise that enthusiasm for institutional religion is a fairly specialised sport these days.

The research showed that this audience wanted from religious broadcasting whatever would enhance their personal happiness, provide the "feel-good factor" and increase their experience of personal well-being. There was no interest in programmes which explored issues of social justice. There was no interest in deep questions of life and death. Or even in questions of meaning.

But how can the church preach the Gospel without addressing questions of life and death? Christians believe that what was unique about Jesus of Nazareth was his death on the cross, and so anything

Christians say about their Lord must be capable of being said through the mouth of the crucified Christ. There is comfort in the Christian faith but we short-change the Gospel if we make it all flabby contentment.

Political Engagement

Time for another story and a picture of wild ducks, from Kierkegaard.

> A wild duck flew with his mates northwards across Europe in the springtime, and on the flight he came down in a barnyard in Denmark where there were some tame ducks. He ate, and enjoyed some of their corn, and stayed – first for an hour, and then for a day, and then for a week, and then for a month, and finally, because he liked the good fare and the safety of the barnyard, he stayed all summer. But one autumn day, when his wild mates were winging their way southward again, they passed over the barnyard, and their mate heard their cries. It stirred him with a strange thrill of joy and delight; and, flapping his wings, he rose in the air to join his old comrades in their flight to the land of summer. But he found that his good fare had made him so soft and heavy that he could rise no higher than the eaves of the barn. So he sank back again to the barnyard and said to himself 'Oh well, my life is safe here and the fare is good.' Every spring, and again in every autumn, when the wild ducks flew over his barnyard, and he heard their honking cry, his eye gleamed for a moment and he began to lift his wings and would have loved to have joined his mates. But the time came when the wild ducks flew over him and uttered their cry and he paid not the slightest attention to them.
>
> Soren Kierkegaard, Danish philosopher

A parable of the dangers of contentment. And of the temptations of being diverted from the course of our real purpose as the church, a purpose famously characterised by Archbishop Temple as being for the sake of those who are not our members. And that brings us to the thrilling and demanding world of political commentary.

"Who needs the church?" The answer given by Gerald Priestland, the journalist, was: "The man in the street needs the church. The greatest single reason why the man in the street needs the church is that he needs an alternative source of criticism and comment on the secular world. He needs the prophecy – the speaking forth – that the church has always given: a dangerous activity, perhaps, for it can always lapse into second rate politics, but it has to be done".

Several points here: the church's prophetic role as a civic institution, the dangers of second-rate politics and the nature of the alternative comment.

I count myself tremendously privileged to have been Convener of the Church and Nation Committee of the Church of Scotland for four years, at the time when the new Scottish Parliament was being brought into being. That is the committee that advises our General Assembly on political matters. It was a kind of institutionalised prophecy. It offered a critique of policy from a Christian perspective, it amplified the concerns of those whose voices were weak or on the margins, and it used the international reach of the church to widen the scope of concern away from Scotland. The Committee did its best to tap into the expertise of members of the church to ensure that its reports were well researched, timely and focussed on issues that mattered for people who needed others to amplify their voices and draw attention to their experiences, or on issues that had important consequences for the health and future of the community. Over the years, we presented reports on the minimum wage, land reform, open cast mining, the war in Kosovo and so on.

Before the advent of the Parliament, which the Assembly consistently advocated, it was said that the Church and Nation debates offered the people of Scotland, wider than the membership of the Kirk, a forum that was lacking in the democracy of the day. It was an example of a strong civil society playing its part in the wider political process and this was welcomed by other players, such as the trades unions, other professional bodies and voluntary organisations.

That has changed now that the Parliament carries the representative responsibilities for the country. There has been less enthusiasm for civic institutions to weigh into the debate. What has been called the old civil society, typified by the minister, the teacher, the lawyer and the doctor, the professionals who shared a common view of what was good for you, is less regarded than it was. The Parliamentarians now tend to want to reach over that consensus to the individual voter, and the diversity of civil society, rather than its commonality, is more politically prized.

But the churches continue their critique and exercise it at varying levels. People have been appointed to brief church members about exactly what is happening in the Parliament, how to get further information, as well as to share stimulating theological comment on some of the issues of the moment. The Scottish Churches' Parliamentary Office is based on a similar enterprise in Brussels that helps churches in Europe to have an intelligent dialogue with the European Union on matters of poverty, or the environment, or development concerns. It's hard, intense work, and there are never enough resources committed to it. I often feel that the churches are burdened with the opportunities for political engagement, which are far more than they have the capacity to utilise.

The expectation that the churches will make a well honed contribution to political debate is engrained in our culture in Scotland. But for some people, the mark of authenticity in the church's voice is intemperate anger at the injustices of our day. The contrast between the carefully researched report and the fiery burst of passion lurks close beneath the surface. As it always has done.

I'm indebted to my friend and Moderator's chaplain, Johnston McKay for drawing my attention to an observation about Robert Burns, who was a Professor in this college in the nineteenth century. He had been minister of St George's Church in Paisley, and his contemporary in Paisley Abbey was Patrick Brewster. Confronted with issues of politics, economics and poverty, Brewster preached sermons with grand oratorical flourishes about the needs of the poor. He was dubbed "a fiery salamander". But Robert Burns undertook a historical survey of the poor laws, and argued from that basis that the support for the poor was unjust. Burns' book, *Historical Dissertations on the Law and Practice of Great Britain, and particularly of Scotland, with regard to the Poor*, is still examined by law students at Glasgow University, while the sermons of Patrick Brewster are seldom read.

Political engagement can, of course, take many forms. The homework has to be done and it can pay off in the careful advocacy of a case. Yet often what breaks through in the church's dialogue with politicians are the moments when the careful homework is set aside and the church speaks in its own language of love and forgiveness, of hope and generosity.

It's tantalising work. Because you are walking a tightrope between the pragmatism of political calculation and the extravagant, anarchic gospel vision. Between the need to make things work and the impossibility of the promised kingdom, where, as R S Thomas says,:

> There are quite different things going on:
> Festivals at which the poor man
> Is king and the consumptive is
> Healed; mirrors in which the blind look
> At themselves and love looks at them
> Back; and industry is for mending
> The bent bones and the minds fractured
> By life.

RS Thomas, the Bright Field, Collected Poems

The Foolishness of the Possible

It all sounds rather foolish.

There is a lovely story which the former Bishop of Durham. David Jenkins likes to tell, of how after he received the invitation to be Bishop of Durham, he went to the island of Lindisfarne to work out whether or not he wanted to accept or not. He was undecided. He knew he might be controversial. He might get into trouble, as he did, with both church and politicians for his outspoken views. As he was thinking it over he was walking along a path which came to a kind of crossroads. He could go one way or another. But a little further up one of the paths what looked like a piece of paper fluttering on the ground caught his attention; so he went that way. As he got closer he realised that what had caught his attention was, in fact, a playing card. It was lying face downwards, but before he picked it up he knew which card it was. It was the joker. And his mind was made up.

Kings and queens long ago didn't keep jokers, jesters, fools, because they wanted to be amused. Fools weren't comedians. They belonged to the court, but they weren't part of the court's intrigue. Fools weren't party to the scheming and the plotting, the manoeuvring and the manipulation, the jockeying for position and the struggle for power. And so fools saw things that other people didn't see; and said things that other people couldn't say. They got away with speaking the truth. Indeed fools were the only people who could be trusted to speak the truth because everyone knew the fool had no axe to grind; after all, he was just a fool.

The church has the strength of being an honest broker. If it plays a straight political game, conforming to the categories of others and signing up to being another lobby group, it will be taken seriously and many people will be grateful for the church in that role. I remember meeting a representative of Shelter, the homelessness charity, just after an Assembly when we had offered a report, using material from Shelter itself. I admitted this but he said "When the church says these things, people listen. When we say it, they comment 'They would say that, wouldn't they'" Our independence is a precious bonus.

But what happens when we try to speak in our own terms, create our own categories for debate? Talk about vulnerability being a strength, about sacrificial giving or the richness of simplicity? The danger is that people don't listen, don't take you seriously. Kierkegaard again:

> "A circus proprietor discovered that the big tent was on fire, and he called on of his employees and said 'Go into the middle of the circus ring and tell the people that the tent is on fire and they must get out as quickly as they can.' The man went, but in a little while he came back saying 'They would not listen to me! They only laughed at

me!' 'Go again' said the proprietor, 'and make them listen! Say to them the circus is on fire, flee for your lives!' But again he returned, saying, 'They laughed at me! They refused to listen to me!' Because the man whom the circus proprietor had sent was the clown; and no one took the clown seriously".

What we need to try and capture is a serious kind of foolishness. The foolishness of those who refuse to conform to the limits of the possible.

Jesus of Nazareth refused to allow people to conform to the limits of the possible. He talked about and practised absurdities like loving your enemies; he cherished the unlovable and the unlovely; and he claimed that forgiving and being forgiven is what makes us human.

"Stretch out your hand" he says to a man who has never had the use of his arm. "Get up and walk" he says to a man who has never taken a step in his life. "Join me in Galilee" he says to men and women who were paralysed by fear, having seen the death he died.

The public space can be a harsh one and drab. Understandably so because the wounds and injustices of our day cause pain and despair. Poverty that is stubbornly resistant to its eradication, reversion to conflict as an acceptable tool of international policy, rising sea levels and environmental roulette. It calls for the wisdom of more than the political world to address the crisis.

Politics may see itself as the art of the possible, yet too often it serves to entrench the impossibility of transformation because of its limited horizons. What we can offer is a perspective of hope, hope that sees the world through eyes bathed in the upside down riches of the

Kingdom, and the generosity of a loving creator. Hope that can be communicated in ways that lift the spirit and give rein to the imagination so that we can stretch the limits of the possible on behalf of the world that God still loves. We have an exciting time ahead of us.

March 7th 2005, Knox College Toronto.

CONNECT

The title "Connect" is a very good title for the Church of Scotland to have for its Guild Annual Meeting. And that is because, in many ways, the Church of Scotland is increasingly becoming known as the "Church without Walls" church. And, insofar as walls divide people, then presumably a Church without Walls is a church that is continually making the connections between people, between parts of its work, between itself and the parts of the community that surround it.

Over the last few months, you've sent me as Moderator to attend the Assemblies of our sister churches in Ireland, England and Wales. It's been a very revealing experience. We're all addressing the same kinds of things. Trying to work out what the relationship should be between ministry and mission; looking at the structures of the church; commissioning studies on what membership means. And this is understandable because we're all set in the same kinds of communities and so we're faced with many of the same dilemmas and opportunities.

But what I also found interesting was that each church seemed to have a catch-phrase of its own. The new Irish Moderator had taken as his theme for the year *Live a Life of Love* and that was a phrase which dominated the Assembly. The United Reformed Church was busy trying to *Catch the Vision* as it searched for a shape and an ethos with which to face up to the challenges of the 21st century.

But it was in the Presbyterian Church of Wales, *Moving Forward*, that we were accorded the compliment by the retiring Moderator of picking up our *Church without Walls* theme in his closing address. It sparked in him a comparison with a particular passage in *Murder in the Cathedral* by T S Eliot. At the high point of the drama, where four knights sent by the king to kill Thomas Beckett are about to enter the cathedral, the reaction of the priests is to bar the door. But the Archbishop answers:

> Unbar the door! Throw open the doors!
> I will not have the house of prayer, the church of Christ,
> The sanctuary, turned into a fortress.
> The Church shall protect her own, in her own way, not
> As oak and stone; oak and stone decay,
> Give no stay, but the Church shall endure.
> The church shall be open, even to our enemies.
> Open the door!

Powerful stuff! You might be ready to point out that Thomas was quickly dispatched after this, but of course the church did endure and has been inspired by his example.

It's often been said that the phrase "Church without Walls" has captured people's imagination far more successfully than the content of the report might have led one to expect. It slips into conversations as a wee corrective to attitudes that are too defensive or to energies being directed towards maintenance of a structure which in the end of the day is supposed to be enabling rather than constricting. And I think that's a good thing. In these days of slogans and logos, if the Church of Scotland is to have a symbol designed for the 21st century, then "Church without Walls" is one that I'd be proud of.

For me, the Gospel of Jesus Christ is liberating and welcoming. It's a pearl of great price to offer the rest of the world and it's something that we can be relaxed about offering, confident that it will survive the challenges and distortions we expose it to. It's the Gospel which is the heart of our security, not a status or a privilege that we have to be defensive about.

I think that one of the things that makes me proud of the phrase "Church without Walls" and the model that it offers is that it's coming at a time that's fragile for the church. There's a lot of suspicion of religion at official levels just now. Membership is falling. Most of the time, the dominant culture is unapologetic about denying any place to things spiritual or religious. And that's precisely the kind of circumstance in which many people would think they were justified in putting up the walls rather than trying to bring them down.

That's what's happening in Israel, where that vast Security Wall is being put up in order to try to keep apart the Palestinians and the Israelis. "It's for our security. It's because we're threatened." It's what happens when big states are threatened; when America reacts to terrorism with the war on terror and with mechanisms for protecting American security that curtail human freedom and infringe human rights. It's what's been happening in Belfast for a long time. In the papers this week, there was a report of what is poignantly described as a peace line in Belfast. It describes one of the streets, Manor Street, as being now bisected by peace lines of railings, steel walls and fenced-in open ground that provides several layers of separation between Protestant and Catholic. When we feel insecure, we tend to build walls, rather than pull them down.

And yet, Jesus didn't shut himself off from trouble or confine his time and his attention to a small group of like-minded friends. He was continually reaching out, across the barriers of social respectability, stigma and difference to make the connection with the real, genuine child of God on the other side. And his church must do the same. It seems to me that any church that turns people away or makes them feel that they're not good enough to be part of their fellowship is a church that's lost the plot. It's by connecting with other people that we learn more about ourselves, that we're more likely to meet Christ, that we're more likely to discover the true, liberating love that is the heartbeat of the Gospel.

Last week, there was an exhibition in my home church of pictures of Jesus that had been painted by artists from all round the world – Mongolia, the Solomon Islands, Japan. They produced an array of images that challenged our very traditional picture of Jesus. There was a particularly telling series of pictures by the Palestinian artist Zaki Baboun who comes from Bethlehem. They portrayed Jesus fairly traditionally as a shepherd. But two of them included a picture of the Israeli Separation Wall, depicted as a series of large slabs, cutting through the towns and olive groves. In the second of these, Jesus is walking along the wall and, as he does so, the slabs of the wall fall like a row of dominoes, turning the wall into a path.

What a wonderful image that is! It represents the heart of the Christian message as being one of encounter, healing and reconciliation. One where the dividing walls are torn down and turned into paths where people can meet, share their stories and continue on their way together.

It reminds me of one of the most powerful experiences I've had while representing the church. That was fifteen years ago, in 1989, when I was a delegate to the First European Ecumenical Assembly in Basel, in Switzerland. If you remember, that was at a time when Europe was divided by another wall, the Berlin Wall, trying to keep East and West apart. As a result of very careful negotiation, delegates from churches in Eastern Europe had been enabled to come to the Assembly and join those of us from the West for a fantastic week of celebration, of reflection and of commitment.

At one point, members of the Assembly were walking from the

Cathedral in Basel to the place where the Assembly was being held, and we were crossing the Rhine. At that point, the Rhine is quite broad and, as we looked, we saw that a tightrope had been slung across the Rhine from the tops of high buildings on either side. As we watched, we realised that there were two tightrope walkers, who were in fact a father and his son, starting out, one from each side. They had great long balancing poles and slowly they walked towards each other. When they got to the centre of the tightrope, high above the Rhine, they sat down. Easier said than done, as you can imagine. They talked to each other for a while and then they both got up and both walked, in the same direction this time, towards one of the sides.

As a little illustration of the journey of healing and reconciliation this was a powerful one. It represents so beautifully the simplicity of the journey, the riskiness of it, and the patience that is required, both to train for that kind of journey and also to see it safely through.

We set high standards for ourselves when we describe ourselves as a Church without Walls. We make ourselves vulnerable, vulnerable to other people finding out things about ourselves that we don't want them to find out or even that we don't want to admit about ourselves. Vulnerable to failure. But there is a strength in that very vulnerability.

As people in the church have been reflecting on the significance of September 11th, they have drawn attention to the way in which America, and by extension the rest of the Western world, was shown to be very vulnerable on that occasion. Yet Christian thinkers on this, in consultations brought together by the World Council of Churches which I attended, have noted that vulnerability is part of the human condition. To be invulnerable is to be, not super-human but inhuman. And as we face that vulnerability within ourselves, we also see it as a strength. Because we recognise in that our dependence on God and our dependence on each other. And, through that recognition, we have an opportunity to grow stronger in ways that will last.

By making the connections with each other, we also see how partial our own perspective is. My own background has been very strongly involved in ecumenical work where I have been greatly strengthened and enriched by meeting people from other traditions. And in meeting these other traditions, I realise both the shortcomings of my own, but, by comparison with theirs, I also begin to learn what the truly important things are in the Church of Scotland Presbyterian tradition that I'm proud to hang on to.

So let's take our image of the Church without Walls seriously. As long as we in the church shut ourselves up behind defensive walls of status, of an arrogant self-sufficiency, of the spurious safety of the dead parts of our tradition, then we have very little to offer those parts of our community and the wider world that are hurting as they cower behind their Separation Walls, or peace lines. As they hide themselves away because they're ashamed of their poverty. As they feel that they're stigmatised because of their mental health problems. Or as they lie bewildered in a detention centre, wondering if this is the asylum they were seeking. Jesus would have been beside them. And that's where we should be as well.

Guild Annual Meeting, 28th August 2004, Glasgow.

SENDING OUT

Almighty and ever living God
We come before you at the end of our week together
We've received reports
Scrutinised people's work
Taken decisions
Given instructions
We've caught up with old friends and made new ones
We've touched the lives of people here in this building and
far from it
We give you thanks for your energising presence with us
And pray that what we have done will advance your
Kingdom

Eternal Word, made flesh and sent to dwell among us
All week, we have been engulfed with words
We know that, among them, you have been speaking to us
We fear that
      What you have said has gone unnoticed
         as we have pursued our own agenda
      what you have said has become part of the white
      noise
         of extravagant claims and well meant promises
what you have said has been mangled
      through our misunderstanding of its precious
      kernel
Grant us, we pray,
      Hearts in which your word can take root
      Ears that hear you speaking to us
      And lives that are full of your gracious love

Lord Jesus
Stay with us, we pray,

As we leave this place and travel home
Stay with us and disturb us with memories of pain and injustice

That lead us forward into a deeper awareness of your love and compassion
Stay with us and remind us of moments of peace and inspiration

And show us how they can be rekindled in our lives and the lives of others
Guide us, nurture us, and keep us, this night and always.
We ask it in your name, Amen.

Friday May 21st at the closing of the General Assembly 2004.

ACKNOWLEDGEMENTS

The publishers gratefully acknowledge permission to reproduce extracts from the following:

Yehuda Amichai, *The Selected Poetry of Yehuda Amichai* (edited and translated by Chana and Stephen Bloch, copyright 1996) The Regents of the University of California

Walter Brueggeman, *Inscribing the Text: Sermons and Prayers of Walter Brueggeman* copyright 2004 published by Augsburg Fortress (www.augsburgfortress.org). Reprinted with permission.

Donald Davie, Ordinary God from *To Scorch or Freeze* published by Carcanet Press Ltd

George Macleod, from the prayer A Chaos of Uncalculating Love, copyright Wild Goose Publications, from *The Whole Earth Shall Cry Glory*, Wild Goose Publications, Glasgow (www.ionabooks.com).

Robert Runcie, *Windows into God,* published by SPCK, London

TS Eliot, Murder in the Cathedral, *The Poems and Plays of TS Eliot*, published by Faber & Faber

RS Thomas, Kneeling, The Bright Field, The Kingdom from *Collected Poems 1945 – 1990* published by JM Dent, London 1993

Derick Thomson, *Plundering the Harp: Collected Poems 1940 – 1970* published by Macdonald, 1982

Iain Crichton Smith, I build an orange house from *Selected Poems* published by Carcanet Press Ltd

Other titles available:

Praying on the Edge
By Bryan Owen
Covenanters

An excellent bible based study providing information about human rights situations the world over. This book encourages and empowers the reader to bring Jesus' light into dark places through a sensible plan of action including group study and prayer. Perfect for use during Lent or at any time of year.
ISBN 1905022026 softback price £10.95 (Hardback edition also available, contact us for details)

Keeping it Cheery
Bridgeton Youth Club (Glasgow) remembered
By Bill Shackleton
Covenanters

Memoirs of Glasgow's East End evoke a passionate response whenever they are published. *Keeping It Cheery* will be no exception. Harry Reid contributes a spirited foreword to this the first entire book written by the incorrigibly irreverent Bill Shackleton - who recalls 50 years of ministry in stories of people and places that will have you rolling in the aisles. This book has been described by 'a great read' by Sally Magnusson.
ISBN 1905022000 softback price £14.95
Hardback available! ISBN 1 905022 01 8 price £27.95

Gaun Yersel Moses
A lighthearted trip through the Old Testament in Glaswegian Verse
By Tom C White

The Old Testament as you've never seen it before - in Glaswegian rhyming verse! A must-read for all in need of a shot of Scotch...
ISBN 1904325076 £4.99

Parable Patter
A light-hearted trip through the New Testament in Glaswegian verse
By Tom C. White

Tom White brings the parables of Jesus into Glaswegian rhyming verse. Witty and contemporary and not a little riotous in places, these stories will communicate eternal truths in a really accessible way. Fun for everyone.
ISBN 1904325157 £4.99

All books available from Booksource 08702 402 182 or from www.covenanters.co.uk